Preface

Aim

The aim of the *Essential Elements* series is to provide course support material covering the main subject areas of HND/C Business Studies and equivalent level courses at a price that students can afford. Students can select titles to suit the requirements of their own particular courses whether BTEC Certificate in Business Administration, Certificate in Marketing, IPS Foundation, Institute of Bankers, Access to Business Studies, Institute of Personnel Management, or other appropriate undergraduate and professional courses.

Many courses now have a modular structure, i.e. individual subjects are taught in a relatively short period of, say, 10 to 12 weeks. The *Essential Elements* series meets the need for material which can be built into the students' study programmes and used for directed self-study. All the texts, therefore, include activities with answers for students' self-assessment, activities for lecturer-assessment, and references to further reading.

The series is a joint venture between DP Publications and South Birmingham College.

How to use the series

All the books in the series are intended to be used as workbooks and provide approximately 70 hours of study material. Each text covers the essential elements of that subject, so that the core of any course at this level is covered, leaving the lecturer to add supplementary material if required. All have the following features:

☐ **In-text activities,** which aim to promote understanding of the principles, and are set at frequent intervals in the text. The solutions add to the student's knowledge, as well as providing an introduction to the next learning point.

☐ **End of chapter exercises,** some of which are intended for self-assessment by the student (these have solutions at the back of the book). Others are suitable for setting by the lecturer and answers or marking guides are provided in the Lecturers' Supplement. These exercises include progress and review questions, multiple choice questions, which test specific knowledge and allow rapid marking, practice questions, questions for advanced students, and assignments.

☐ **Further reading references** for students who wish to follow up particular topics in more depth.

☐ **Lecturers' Supplement,** which is available free of charge to lecturers adopting the book as a course text. It includes answers or guides to marking to help with student assessment.

Essential Elements of Quantitative Methods follows on from Business Statistics in the same series and students will be assumed to have this knowledge.

Other titles in the series

Available 1994: Business Economics, Business Planning and Policy, Business Statistics, Management Accounting, Marketing.

Available 1995: Business Law, Human Resource Management, Management Information Systems, Operations Management.

Contents

Essential Elements of

Quantitative Methods

Les Oakshott BSc (Hons), MSc, PGCE

Senior lecturer in the Department of Mathematical Sciences, University of the West of England, Bristol

Series adviser: Bob Cudmore BEd, MBA, Head of Management and Professional Studies Division, South Birmingham College

Technical adviser: David Holden BA (Hons), MSc, PGCE, South Birmingham College

Pub...
DP...
199...

Library

CHESTER COLLEGE

Donation

SOUTH BIRMINGHAM COLLEGE

Acknowledgments

I would like to thank the Central Statistical Office for permission to include figures and tables from their publications.

A CIP catalogue reference for this book is available from the British Library

ISBN 1 85805 098 7

Typeset by KAI Typesetting, 21 Sycamore Rise, Cinderhill, Nottingham

Printed in Great Britain by the Guernsey Press Co. Ltd, Vale, Guernsey

1 Index numbers

1.1 Introduction

An index is a means of comparing changes in some variable, often price, over time. This is particularly useful when there are many items involved and the prices and quantities are in different units. The most well known index is the retail price index. This index compares the price of a 'basket' of goods from one month to another and is used as a measure of inflation. This chapter looks at the construction and use of different types of indices.

At the end of this chapter you should be able to:

❐ Calculate a simple one item index

❐ Calculate the Laspeyres' index

❐ Calculate the Paasche's index

❐ Understand how the retail price index is calculated and be able to use it to deflate financial data.

1.2 Simple indices

Example 1

The price of an item and quantity sold have varied over the past 5 years as follows:

Year	Price	Quantity
1989	£6.00	2500
1990	£6.20	3500
1991	£5.52	3800
1992	£6.95	2000
1993	£8.82	3200

Since 1989 the item has gone up in price by £2.82. But how much has it gone up relative to the price in 1989? If 1989 is used as a base then it is possible to compare changes in price with this base. The base is given a value of 100 so that a price increase would result in value above 100 while a price decrease would result in a value less than 100. If £6 is equivalent to 100 then £8.82 is equivalent to:

$$\frac{100}{6} \times 8.82 = 147$$

The value 147 is called the price index and 1989 is the base year. If p_n represents the current year (year 'n') and p_0 represents the base year then the price index is:

$$\frac{100}{p_0} \times p_n$$

Or normally it is expressed as:

$$\frac{p_n}{p_0} \times 100$$

Activity 1

Using the data in Example 1 calculate the price index for each year.

The table you should have obtained is as follows:

Year	Price Index
1989	100
1990	103
1991	92
1992	116
1993	147

(The figures have been rounded to the nearest whole number)

As well as price the quantity sold has varied over the year so a quantity index could also be calculated. If q_n represents the current year and q_0 represents the base year the quantity index is given by:

$$\frac{q_n}{q_0} \times 100$$

So the quantity index for 1993 using 1989 as the base year is:

$$\frac{3200}{2500} \times 100 = 128$$

Activity 2

Calculate the quantity index for each year.

You should have obtained the following table:

Year	Quantity Index
1989	100
1990	140
1991	152
1992	80
1993	128

It is rare to calculate an index for just one item, usually you will have several items as seen in Example 2 below.

Example 2

The resources used in the manufacture of Delta glass fibre boats include resin, glass fibre mat and labour. The price of each of these resources varies and have been as follows:

Item	1991	1992	1993
Resin	£0.25/l	£0.20/l	£0.18/l
Mat	£0.16/m²	£0.16/m²	£0.20/m²
Labour	£5.50/hour	£5.85/hour	£8.30/hour

Activity 3

Calculate the index for each item using 1991 as the base year.

You should have obtained the following table:

Item	1991	1992	1993
Resin	100	80	72
Mat	100	100	125
Labour	100	106	151

You can see that the index for resin has shown a decrease while labour has shown the largest increase. But what does this tell you about the cost of production? Is it possible to combine the data in some way so that an aggregate index can be obtained.

Activity 4

Could you obtain an aggregate index simply by adding the prices together for each year?

There are two problems with this approach. First the items are in different units, you have litres, square metres and hours. And secondly the importance of each item might be different. If labour is the dominant cost then the aggregate index should reflect this fact. To overcome these problems each item is weighted according to its importance. When this is done you have a weighted aggregate index.

1.3 Weighted aggregate indices

In order to weight an index it is necessary to have information on the importance of each item. For the boat example this could be done by recording the quantities used in its production

Example 3

The quantities required in the production of a boat varies from year to year as production methods change. This can be seen in the table below.

Item	1991	1992	1993
Resin	50 l	48 l	48 l
Mat	200 m²	210 m²	215 m²
Labour	30 hours	27 hours	23 hours

Activity 5

How might you use the information in Examples 2 and 3 to create an aggregate index?

Since price × quantity equals the cost of that item the aggregate index could be obtained as:

$$\frac{\text{Total cost of production at current prices}}{\text{Total cost of production at base year prices}}$$

There is however one problem with this definition. What quantities should we use? Both price and quantities have varied from year to year and for comparison purposes we need to use the same quantities for the numerator and denominator of the index. The choice is to use either the base year quantities or the current year quantities. When you use the former you have a base weighted or Laspeyres' index and when you use the latter you have a current weighted or Paasche's index.

1.3.1 Laspeyres' index

The definition of the Laspeyres' index is:

$$\frac{\text{Total cost of base year quantities at current prices}}{\text{Total cost of base year quantities at base year prices}}$$

Using p to represent price and q to represent quantity this definition can be expressed as:

Sum of current prices times base quantities

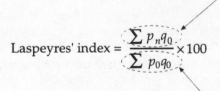

$$\text{Laspeyres' index} = \frac{\sum p_n q_0}{\sum p_0 q_0} \times 100$$

Sum of base prices times base quantities

In order to calculate this index for the boat example you may find it useful to write the data from Examples 2 and 3 into another table as follows:

Item	1991 Price	1991 Qty	1992 Price	1992 Qty	1993 Price	1993 Qty
Resin	£0.25	50	£0.20	48	£0.18	48
Mat	£0.16	200	£0.16	210	£0.20	215
Labour	£5.50	30	£5.85	27	£8.30	23

Each year needs to be calculated separately. For 1992 the calculations are as follows:

p_0	q_0	p_n	$p_0 q_0$	$p_n q_0$
0.25	50	0.20	12.5	10.0
0.16	200	0.16	32.0	32.0
5.50	30	5.85	165.0	175.5
		Sum	**209.5**	**217.5**

So Laspeyres' index for 1992 $= \dfrac{217.5}{209.5} \times 100 = 103.8$

Repeating this procedure for 1993:

p_0	q_0	p_n	$p_0 q_0$	$p_n q_0$
0.25	50	0.18	12.5	9
0.16	200	0.20	32.0	40
5.50	30	8.30	165.0	249
		Sum	**209.5**	**298**

So Laspeyres' index for 1993 $= \dfrac{298}{209.5} \times 100 = 142.2$

You can see from these calculations that there has been a dramatic increase in the index from 1992 to 1993. This was due to the large increase in labour costs that took place during this period.

1.3.2 Paasche's index

The definition of Paasche's index is:

Sum of current prices times current quantities

$$\text{Paasche's index} = \frac{\sum p_n q_n}{\sum p_0 q_n} \times 100$$

Sum of base prices times current quantities

A table can again be used in the calculation. For 1992 the figures are:

p_0	q_n	p_n	$p_0 q_n$	$p_n q_n$
0.25	48	0.20	12.0	9.6
0.16	210	0.16	33.6	33.6
5.50	27	5.85	148.5	158.0
		Sum	**194.1**	**201.2**

So Paasche's index for 1992 $= \dfrac{201.2}{194.1} \times 100 = 103.7$

If you repeat these calculations for 1993 you should find that the sum of $p_0 q_n$ is 172.9 and the sum of $p_n q_n$ is 242.5. So Paasche's index for 1993 is:

$$\frac{242.5}{172.9} \times 100 = 140.3$$

Both indices give similar results for this data and in general there will not be a great difference between the two unless the weights (quantities) are very different. The table below summarises the advantages and disadvantages of each index.

	Laspeyres' index	*Paasche's index*
Ease of calculation	Denominator only calculated once	Denominator recalculated each year
Quantities required each year	No, only base quantities required	Yes
Comparability	Direct comparison from year to year	No direct comparison
Accuracy	Weights quickly become out of date	Reflects consumption patterns in current year

In practise the Laspeyres' index is the most commonly used index and the base year is redefined at regular intervals. When the base year is redefined it is a good idea to recalculate the index for previous years. For example, in the table below the base year was 1985 but it has been decided to change the base year to 1993.

1985	1986	1987	1988	1989	1990	1991	1992	1993
100	105.6	108.9	121.2	142.3	145.1	147.9	148.8	153.1

The Index in 1985 becomes

$$\frac{100}{153.1} \times 100 = 65.3$$

Activity 8

Calculate the index for each subsequent year.

You should have obtained the following table.

1985	1986	1987	1988	1989	1990	1991	1992	1993
65.3	69.0	71.1	79.2	92.9	94.8	96.6	97.2	100

1.4 Retail price index

Unless you live on a desert island you almost certainly have come across the retail price index or RPI. This measures the change in the price of a 'basket' of goods and is used to measure the level of domestic inflation. This index covers some 600 or so items divided into 11 groups. Each group and each item within a group is given a weight that is designed to reflect the importance of that item. The weights are updated annually by the Family expenditure survey and prices of this basket of goods is checked each month.

The RPI can be used to compute the real change in earnings or expenditure.

Example 4

A company's turnover (in £m's) since 1987 has been as follows:

1987	1988	1989	1990	1991	1992
2.3	3.3	4.1	4.2	4.4	4.7

It looks as if turnover has been steadily increasing but at the same time the RPI has also been increasing. The value of the RPI since 1987 has been as follows:

1987	1988	1989	1990	1991	1992
101.9	106.9	115.2	126.1	133.5	138.5

(Source: Monthly Digest of Statistics)

To calculate the real turnover the turnover figures are *deflated* as follows:

1988: $3.3 \times \dfrac{101.9}{106.9} = 3.14$ so a turnover of £3.3m is equivalent to £3.1m at 1987 prices.

Activity 9

Calculate the real turnover for the remainder of the years.

You should have obtained the table below:

1987	1988	1989	1990	1991	1992
2.3	3.1	3.6	3.4	3.4	3.5

The picture is now one of increasing turnover until 1989 and then a drop before partially recovering in 1992. This can be seen better in the graph below.

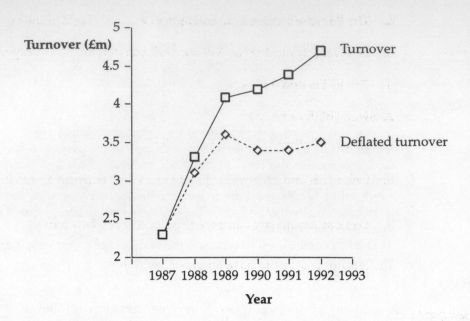

Figure 1

1.5 Summary

This chapter has introduced you to the idea of a index. For a single item or variable a simple index can be used but if you are monitoring several items then it is necessary to use a weighted aggregate index. There are two main weighted indices. These are Laspeyres' index, which is a base weighted index and Paasche's index, which is a current weighted index. The Laspeyres' index is easier to use but soon gets out of date, while the Paasche's index reflects consumption patterns in the current year. The retail price index uses consumption patterns as weights and are derived from a family expenditure survey. The RPI is used as a measure of inflation and allows financial data to be deflated.

1.6 Further reading

Morris, C, *Quantitative Approaches in Business Studies*, Pitman, 1993, Chapter 6

Harper, W, *Statistics, M & E Handbook Series*, Pitman, 1991, Chapter 16.

Francis, A, *Business Mathematics and Statistics*, DP Publications, 1993, Chapter 5

1.7 Exercises

Progress questions

These question have been designed to help you remember the key points in this chapter. The answers to these questions are given in Appendix 1, page 108.

Give the missing word in each case:

1. The base year has an index of ....

2. A simple index is where you have only .... item or variable to monitor.

3. The Laspeyres' index is an example of a .... weighted index.

4. The Paasche's index is an example of a .... weighted index.

5. The weights used in the RPI are derived from the .... expenditure survey.

6. The RPI is updated each ....

Answer TRUE or FALSE:

7. Laspeyres' index is easier to calculate.

   True ☐ False ☐

8. Laspeyres' index requires quantities as well as prices to be obtained each year.

   True ☐ False ☐

9. You cannot directly compare years with Paasche's index.

   True ☐ False ☐

10. It is not possible to have an index below 100.

   True ☐ False ☐

Review questions

These questions have been designed to help you check your comprehension of the key points in this chapter. You may wish to look further than this chapter in order to answer them fully. You will find the reading list useful in this respect. You can check the essential elements of your answers by referring to the appropriate section.

11. What are the essential differences between Laspeyres' index and Paasche's index? (Section 1.3)

12. What weights are used in the RPI index and how are they obtained? (Section 1.4)

13. What is meant by the term 'deflated figures' and what is the purpose of it? (Section 1.4)

Multiple choice questions

The answers to these will be given in the Lecturers' Supplement.

Choose the correct statement in the following multiple choice questions.

14. An index increases from 105 to 110. The change in the index is:
   - A 5 points
   - B 4.75 points
   - C 110 points

15. Laspeyre's index uses:
   - A Base year weights
   - B Current year weights
   - C Average expenditure as weights

16. It has been decided to change the base of an index from 1988 to 1993. If the index in 1993 is 148 what would the index in 1988 become after the change?
   - A 100
   - B 32.4
   - C 67.6
   - D 148

17. The RPI in 1989 was 115.2 and by 1992 it was 138.5. This represents rise in the price of goods by:

    A   15%

    B   20.2%

    C   23.3%

18. The turnover by a company in 1987 was £54.5m and in 1989 it was £75m. If the RPI has increased from 101.9 in 1987 to 115.2 by 1989, the real change in the turnover has been:

    A   £20.5m

    B   £16m

    C   £18.1m

19. If the price index for bananas was 100 in 1993 and that for apples was 110 then the price of a pound of bananas was:

    A   Less than for apples

    B   More than for apples

    C   Impossible to compare with apples

Practice questions

Answers to these questions will be given in the Lecturers' Supplement.

20. The price and quantity consumed in a normal week of 3 items of food for a family are as follows:

	1990 Price	1990 Qty	1994 Price	1994 Qty
Bread	28p/loaf	6 loaves	38p/loaf	6
Milk	20p/pint	15 pints	29p/pint	12
Tea	96p/packet	1 packet	105p/packet	2

a)   Calculate the Laspeyres' index for 1994 using 1990 as the base year.

b)   Calculate the Paasche's index for 1994 using 1990 as the base year.

21. A person has a portfolio of 4 shares. The price and quantity of shares held between 1987 and 1994 are as follows:

Share	1987 Price	No. held	1994 Price	No. held
Company A	160	200	520	500
Company B	350	650	265	250
Company C	105	600	140	400
Company D	53	100	159	200

a)   Calculate the Laspeyres' index for 1994 using 1987 as the base year.

b)   Calculate the Paasche's index for 1994 using 1987 as the base year.

22. The price of a house in a residential district has fallen from £130,000 in 1987 to £95,000 in 1992. What has been the real drop in price if the retail price index has changed from 101.9 in 1987 to 138.5 in 1992?

23. A company's turnover (in £m's) since 1987 has been as follows:

1987	1988	1989	1990	1991	1992
15.3	10.3	12.1	15.2	24.4	34.7

What has been the real turnover if the value of the RPI for each of these years has been as follows:

1987	1988	1989	1990	1991	1992
101.9	106.9	115.2	126.1	133.5	138.5

Assignment

Answers to this assignment are included in the Lecturers' supplement.

You are to use the library to investigate the composition of the RPI and how it is updated. You should use graphs and diagrams to illustrate its composition and provide examples of how the index is calculated. Discuss how useful this index would be to:

a) To the government as a means of controlling inflation,

b) To a union for wage negotiation purposes, and

c) To a pensioner in deciding how well off they are likely to be next year.

Finally, comment on the accuracy of the index.

2 Investment appraisal

2.1 Introduction

Companies are frequently faced with having to decide between a number of investment opportunities. Since capital is frequently limited a company will want to choose the 'best' project or projects. But what do we mean by 'best' and how can we differentiate between different projects that may look equally attractive? The projects considered in this chapter are those that require an initial capital outlay and then generate income over several years. The life of a project is of paramount importance since a sum of money that will be generated in the future will not be so attractive than money that is available in the present. This chapter looks at several methods that can be used to determine the worth of an investment.

At the end of this chapter you should be able to:

- ❏ Understand the reasons for investment appraisal
- ❏ Select projects on the basis of their payback periods
- ❏ Calculate the Accounting Rate of Return
- ❏ Discount a future sum of money
- ❏ Select projects on the basis of their Net Present Value
- ❏ Calculate the Internal Rate of Return for a project
- ❏ Appreciate the limitations of each method

2.2 Measures of investment worth

You may think that it should be easy to judge the worth of an investment. Surely the larger the profit that will be generated the better? Unfortunately it is not so simple as this as two projects could generate the same total profit but be quite different in the pattern of cash flows. The example below illustrates a typical example.

Example

BAS Holdings specialises in the development of out-of-town shopping centres. It is currently investigating three possible projects and these are located at Andover(A), Bristol(B) and Carlisle(C). The site at Andover and Bristol requires an investment of £4m while the site at Carlisle requires an investment of £5m. Income from rents is guaranteed for up to 5 years, after which time BAS Holdings will transfer ownership to the district council. The net cash flows are given in the table below, where year 0 refers to 'now'.

Year	Andover (£m)	Bristol (£m)	Carlisle (£m)
0	-4.0	-4.0	-5.0
1	1.0	1.5	0.0
2	1.0	2.5	5.0
3	1.0	5.0	1.5
4	1.0	5.0	2.0
5	1.0	0.0	3.0

In the example above the company has to decide which, if any of the projects to accept. Even if all projects are profitable the company may not have the resources to proceed with them all. Perhaps it should compare each project in terms of the profit made at the end of the 5 years (4 years in the case of Bristol).

Activity 1

What is the total profit for each project?

The profit is simply the sum of the cash flows over the life of each project and is as follows:

Year	Andover (£m)	Bristol (£m)	Carlisle (£m)
0	-4.0	-4.0	-5.0
1	1.0	1.5	0.0
2	1.0	2.5	0.5
3	1.0	0.5	1.5
4	1.0	0.5	2.0
5	1.0	0.0	3.0
Profit	1.0	1.0	2.0

On the basis of total profit the Carlisle project is best but this project also has the largest initial investment and income is not generated until year 2. Andover and Bristol give the same profit but notice how differently the earnings are generated; Bristol gives larger cash flows at the start but no earnings are received in year 5, whereas Andover gives a constant flow of earnings for the full 5 years.

You should now appreciate that it is not a simple matter deciding on the best project. There are several methods that can be used to compare projects and these fall into two categories. The first category is often termed 'traditional' and involve accounting procedures that do not take into account the time value of money. The second method involves procedures that discount future sums of money.

2.3 Traditional methods for comparing projects

There are two main methods in this category. These are the Payback method and the Accounting Rate of Return (ARR). The payback method simply tells you how long it takes for the original investment to be repaid.

What are the payback periods for the three projects given in the example?

You should have obtained 4 years for Project 'A', 2 years for project 'B' and 4 years for project 'C'. This indicates that the Bristol project is to be preferred since it takes less time for the original investment to be repaid.

The payback method is an easily understood method and favours projects that generate large cash flows early. This is an advantage since early cash flows will help a company's liquidity and also minimise risks of unforseen problems in the future. However, this method ignores cash flows that are generated after the payback period. For example, with project 'C' large cash flows are generated in years 4 and 5 and this is not taken into account with the payback method.

The Accounting Rate of Return (sometimes called the Return on Capital Employed) is the ratio of average profits to the capital employed. The capital employed sometimes refers to initial capital and sometimes to average capital. There are also variations concerning what constitutes capital and what constitutes profits. The definition used here refers to initial capital and can be expressed as follows:

$$\text{ARR} = \frac{\text{Average profits}}{\text{Initial capital}} \times 100\%$$

Calculate the ARR for all three projects given in the example.

For project 'A' the average profit is £1m and the initial capital employed is £4m so the ARR is:

$$\text{ARR} = \frac{1}{4} \times 100 = 25\%$$

For project 'B' the average profit will again be £1m (the total adds up to £5m – the same as project 'A'). Since the capital employed is £4m the ARR is again 25%.

For project 'C' the average profit is:

$$\frac{0 + 0.5 + 1.5 + 2.0 + 3.0}{5} = 1.4$$

Since the initial capital is £5m the ARR is:

$$\text{ARR} = \frac{1.4}{5} \times 100 = 28\%$$

On the basis of the ARR, project 'C' is the better project.

The ARR is easy to calculate but it has many disadvantages such as not allowing for timing of the cash flows. For example, project 'A' and 'B' are ranked equal even though project 'B' generates larger cash flows in the first two years.

2.4 Discounted cash flow techniques

The disadvantages of the payback and the ARR methods are that they do not take into account the time value of money. If you were offered £1000 now or £1000 in a years time, which would you take? I am sure that you would take £1000 now! However, what would be your decision if you were offered £1000 now or £2000 in a years time. Unless you were desperate for money you would probably prefer to wait a year and get the £2000. These two cases are clear cut. But what would be your decision if you were offered £1000 now or £1100 in a years time? If you could put the money to good use so that after a year you would have more than £1100 then your decision should be to take the £1000 now.

It is clear from this that money in the future is not worth as much as money now so we need some method of discounting future sums of money. In order to understand the idea of discounting it is first necessary to revise the idea of simple and compound interest.

Simple interest is the expression used when interest on a sum of money is calculated on the principal only. This situation occurs when the interest is withdrawn as it is earned.

Activity 4

You decide to invest £8500 in an investment account paying an interest rate of 5% p.a. The interest is paid out to you as it is earned. What interest would you recieve at the end of each year?

The answer to this activity is 5% of £8500, which is £425.

Normally the interest is reinvested so that the interest also earns interest. In this case you would use the expression compound interest.

Activity 5

You again decide to invest £8500 in an investment account paying an interest rate of 5% p.a. This time however, all interest is reinvested. How much would the £8500 have grown to at the end of the 10th year?

The principal at the end of the first year is simply the original principal plus the interest earned. That is:

$$8500 + \frac{5}{100} \times 8500 = 8500\left(1 + \frac{5}{100}\right)$$

This is £8500 × 1.05 = £8925.

The principal at the end of year 2 = principal at the start of year 2 plus the amount of interest received during the year.

That is:
$$8500\left(1 + \frac{5}{100}\right) + 8500\left(1 + \frac{5}{100}\right) \times \frac{5}{100}$$

This can be simplified by noting that the expression $8500\left(1 + \frac{5}{100}\right)$ is common to both terms.

The equation can therefore be *factorised* as follows:

$$8500\left(1+\frac{5}{100}\right)\left(1+\frac{5}{100}\right) = 8500\left(1+\frac{5}{100}\right)^2$$

In general if you invest an initial principal P_0 for n years at an interest rate of $r\%$, the principal at the end of the nth year is:

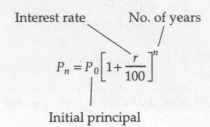

This is called the *compound interest* formula.

So for $P_0 = 8500$, $r = 5$ and $n = 10$ the principal =

$$8500\left(1+\frac{5}{100}\right)^{10} = £13,846$$

Another way of expressing this is that £13,846 in 10 years time at an interest rate of 5% is equivalent to £8500 now. This is quite a useful idea as it allows you to make a judgement on the value of some future sum of money.

Activity 6

You have been promised £10,000 in 5 years time. What would this amount be worth now, assuming an interest rate of 6%?

To solve this problem the compound interest formula can be used in reverse. That is P_n is known and you have to calculate P_0. In this case $n = 5$, $r = 6\%$ and $P_n = 10,000$ and the equation becomes:

$$10,000 = P_0\left(1+\frac{6}{100}\right)^5$$

$$= 1.3382\, P_0$$

Therefore: $P_0 = \dfrac{10,000}{1.3382}$

$$= £7,473$$

Since this calculation will be repeated many times you will find it easier to rearrange the compound interest formula to make P_0 the subject of the formula. That is:

$$P_0 = P_n \times \frac{1}{\left(1+\dfrac{r}{100}\right)^n}$$

The expression:

$$\frac{1}{\left(1+\dfrac{r}{100}\right)^n}$$

is called the *discount factor* and has been tabulated for different values of r and n in Appendix 2, page 114. For example, for $r = 6\%$ and $n = 5$ the discount factor is 0.7473.

So $P_0 = 10000 \times 0.7473$

                   $= £7473$

Activity 7

Discount the sum of £30,000 that is to be received in 4 years time using an interest rate of:

a) 2%

b) 10%.

You should have found that the discount factors for 2% and 10% are 0.9238 and 0.6830 respectively. Therefore the discounted value of £30,000 is:

$30000 \times 0.9238 = £27,714$ at an interest rate of 2%

and $30000 \times 0.6830 = £20,490$ at an interest rate of 10%

2.4.1 Present value

Activity 8

You have been offered either £5000 in 2 years time or £6000 in 3 years time. Which would you accept assuming an interest rate of 5.5%?

This is a slightly different problem in that you are asked to compare a sum of money in 2 years time with a sum of money in 3 years. In order to compare the two amounts you need to have a common base. The easiest method is to find the value now of both amounts. The diagram below explains this more clearly.

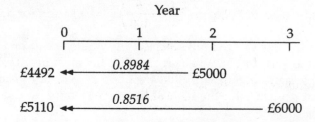

Figure 1

The discount factors are given on top of each arrow and the value at the point of the arrow is the value now of each sum of money. This shows you that £6000 in 3 years time is the better choice since the present value of £6000 is worth more than the present value of £5000 due in 2 years time. This idea of calculating the present value of a sum of money can be extended to the case where a project generates a series of cash flows and the present value of the sum of these cash flows is required. The interest rate that is used is usually called the discount rate and is the cost of capital for the company.

In the case of BAS Holdings the company's discount rate is 8%. Calculate the present value for each of the three projects given in the example.

The calculations are best set out in a table similar to the one below:

Year	Discount Factor	Andover Cash flow (£m)	Andover Present Value	Bristol Cash Flow (£m)	Bristol Present Value	Carlisle Cash Flow (£m)	Carlisle Present Value
0		−4.0		−4.0		−5.0	
1	0.9259	1.0	0.9259	1.5	1.3889	0.0	0.0000
2	0.8574	1.0	0.8574	2.5	2.1435	0.5	0.4287
3	0.7938	1.0	0.7938	0.5	0.3969	1.5	1.1907
4	0.7350	1.0	0.7350	0.5	0.3675	2.0	1.4700
5	0.6806	1.0	0.6806	0.0	0.0000	3.0	2.0418
			3.9927		4.2968		5.1312

From this table you should see that the largest present value is project 'C' with a total cash flow of £5.13m. However, to achieve this, a capital investment of £5m was required, whereas the other two projects only require an investment of £4m. To obtain the profit, the investment should be deducted from the present value and when this is done the result is called the Net Present Value or NPV.

What is the NPV for each of the three projects?

The calculations are: £3.9927 − £4 = −£0.0073m for project A

£4.2968 − £4 = £0.2968m for project B

and   £5.1312 − £5 = £0.1312m for project C

On the basis of the NPV, project 'A' would result in a loss and is therefore not a profitable investment, while project 'B' is the most profitable investment.

When you use NPV to select one project out of many you would simply choose that project with the highest figure. You can also use NPV to make a decision about one project.

In this case your decision should be as follows:

NPV	Decision
Negative	Reject project
Zero	Indifferent
Positive	Accept project

2.4.2 Internal rate of return

The NPV method is a very useful method as it takes into account the timing of a series of cash flows. However, the decision is dependent on the discount rate used – a larger rate will reduce the NPV and could change the decision from accept to reject. An alternative approach is to calculate that discount rate that will give the NPV of zero. This is called the Internal Rate of Return or IRR. If the IRR for a project is greater or equal to the cost of capital for a company, the project would be acceptable, if not the project should be rejected. In the case of BAS Holdings the cost of capital is 8% and any project with an IRR of at least this figure will be acceptable. Calculation of the IRR is not straightforward but an approximate value can be obtained using either a graphical approach or by linear interpolation. For both methods you need to calculate the NPV for two different discount rates. For the greatest accuracy the NPV's should be small, and preferably one should be positive and one negative. For the graphical method these points are plotted on a graph of NPV against discount rate and a line drawn between them. The point where the line crosses the horizontal axis (which represents zero NPV) can then be read from the graph.

Activity 11

Find the IRR for project 'A'.

For project 'A' a discount rate of 8% gave a NPV of –£0.0073m. For most practical purposes this is virtually zero so the IRR is about 8%. However, to get a more accurate answer you could try another discount rate, say 7.5% The calculations for this discount rate are shown below:

Year	Discount Factor	Cash flow (£m)	Present Value
0		–4.0	
1	0.9302	1.0	0.9302
2	0.8653	1.0	0.8653
3	0.8050	1.0	0.8050
4	0.7488	1.0	0.7488
5	0.6966	1.0	0.6966
			4.0459

The NPV is 4.0459 – 4 = £0.0459m. These two values have been plotted on the following graph.

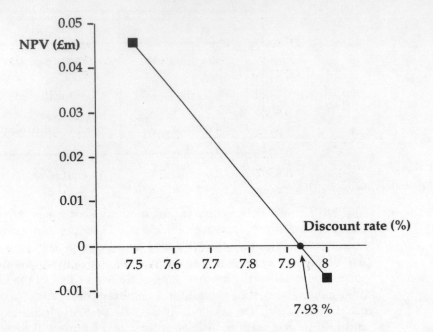

Andover Project

Figure 2

You should find that the line cuts the horizontal axis at 7.92% and this is the value of the IRR for this project. To use the interpolation method the following formula can be used:

$$\text{IRR} = \frac{N_1 r_2 - N_2 r_1}{N_1 - N_2}$$

Where: an NPV of N_1 was obtained using a discount rate of r_1

and: an NPV of N_2 was obtained using a discount rate of r_2

So for $N_1 = 0.0459$, $r_1 = 7.5\%$, $N_2 = -0.0073$ and $r_2 = 8\%$, the IRR is:

$$\text{IRR} = \frac{0.0459 \times 8 - (-0.0073) \times 7.5}{0.0459 - (-0.0073)}$$

$$= \frac{0.42195}{0.0532}$$

$$= 7.93\%$$

Which is the same as the value obtained from the graph.

Activity 12

Find the IRR for project 'B' using the graphical method. (Hint – try discount rates of 11% and 13%).

The calculations for the NPV using discount rates of 11% and 13% are as follows:

Year	Discount Factor (@ 11%)	Cash flow (£m)	Present Value	Discount Factor (@ 13%)	Cash flow (£m)	Present Value
0		−4.0	−4.0			
1	0.9009	1.5	1.3514	0.8850	1.5	1.3274
2	0.8116	2.5	2.0291	0.7831	2.5	1.9579
3	0.7311	0.5	0.3656	0.6931	0.5	0.3465
4	0.6587	0.5	0.3294	0.6133	0.5	0.3067
5	0.5935	0.0	0.0000	0.5428	0.0	0.0000
			0.0754			−0.0615

These NPV values have been plotted on the graph below where you will see that the line joining the two points cuts the axis at a discount rate of about 12.1%

Bristol Project

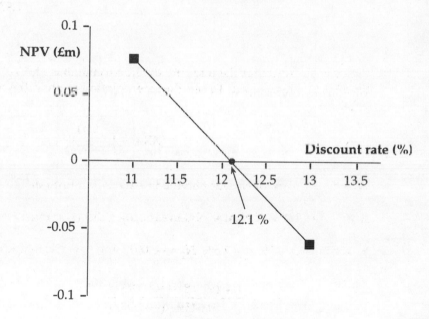

Figure 3

Activity 13

Find the IRR for project 'C' using the formula.

Two rates have been tried, one at 6% which gave a NPV of £0.5304m and one at 8% which gave a NPV of £0.1312m. (You are recommended to do these calculations yourself). Substituting these values into the formula gives you:

$$\frac{0.5304 \times 8 - 0.1312 \times 6}{0.5304 - 0.1312} = \frac{3.456}{0.3992}$$

$$= 8.66\%$$

The results of the IRR calculations agree with the NPV method, that is project 'A' is not profitable while project 'B' appears to be more profitable than project 'C'. The advantage of the IRR method is that it allows you to have a bench mark against which projects can be measured and a rate of return is something that management understand. The disadvantages are that it is more difficult to calculate and does not take into account the absolute value of the cash flows. So on the basis of IRR a project giving a NPV of £100 might look better that a project with a NPV of £1m. There is also the problem that in certain circumstances it is possible for the IRR method to give multiple solutions or no solution at all!

2.5 Summary

This chapter has looked at methods for appraising investments. Two classes of methods were looked at. The first uses traditional accounting procedures such as the payback method and the Accounting Rate of Return while the second category uses discounted cash flow techniques. Each method has its advantages and disadvantages but common sense should tell you that methods that take into account the timing of investments should be better than one that doesn't. To conclude this session it would be useful to summarise the decisions that would be made for choosing the 'best' of the three projects using the four methods described (and a discount rate of 8%).

	Project			
Method	A	B	C	Decision
Payback	4 years	2 years	4 years	B
ARR	25%	25%	28%	C
NPV	-£0.0073m	£0.2968m	£0.1312m	B
IRR	7.92%	12.1%	8.66%	B

2.6 Further reading

Francis, A., *Business Mathematics and Statistics*, DP Publications, 1993, Part 6.

Lucey, T., *Quantitative Techniques*, DP Publications, 1992, Chapter 29.

Peirson, Bird, Brown & Howard, *Business Finance*, McGraw-Hill, 1990, Chapter 4.

2.7 Exercises

Progress questions

These question have been designed to help you remember the key points in this chapter. The answers to these questions are given in Appendix 1, page 108.

Give the missing word in each case:

1. Payback period is the number of years that an investment will take to be

    ....

2. ARR stands for Accounting Rate of ....

3. Simple interest is where the interest is .... as it is earned.

4. Compound interest is where the interest is ....

5. NPV stands for Net .... Value.

Answer true or false.

6. The smaller the ARR the better.

True ☐ False ☐

7. A future amount of money is worth less than it would today.

True ☐ False ☐

8. The NPV of a project depends on the discount rate used.

True ☐ False ☐

9. A project is acceptable if the NPV is less than zero.

True ☐ False ☐

10. A project is acceptable if the IRR is less than the company's cost of capital.

True ☐ False ☐

Review questions

These questions have been designed to help you check your comprehension of the key points in this chapter. You may wish to look further than this chapter in order to answer them fully. You will find the reading list useful in this respect. You can check the essential elements of your answers by referring to the appropriate section.

11. What are the advantages and disadvantages of the Payback method? (Section 2.3).

12. What is the difference between simple and compound interest? (Section 2.4).

13. What are the essential differences between the NPV and IRR methods? (Sections 2.4.1 and 2.4.2).

14. What are the problems with using the IRR method? (Section 2.4.2).

Multiple choice questions

The answers to these will be given in the Lecturers' Supplement.

15. If the average profits over the life of a project was £50,000 and the initial investment was £300,000, the ARR is:
   - A 50%
   - B 16.67%
   - C 0.1667
   - D 30%

16. An investment of £10,000 is made at an interest rate of 5%. If all interest is reinvested the principal at the end of 10 years (to the nearest £) is:

    A £16,289

    B £162,890

    C £15,000

17. The discount factor for a period of 5 years at a discount rate of 6.5% is:

    A 0.7299

    B –0.7299

    C 0.7282

    D 1.7299

Questions 18 to 21 refer to the two projects 'X' and 'Y' given below.

Year	Project X Cash flow (£000's)	Project Y Cash flow (£000's)
0	–100	–110
1	40	0
2	60	30
3	20	100

18. The Payback period for project X is:

    A 1 year

    B 3 years

    C 4 years

19. On the basis of ARR the most profitable project is:

    A Project X

    B Project Y

    C No difference

20. The NPV for project Y at a discount rate of 9% is:

    A £20,000

    B £7531

    C £10,000

21. On the basis of IRR the most profitable project is:

    A Project X

    B Project Y

    C No difference

Practice questions

Answers to these questions will be given in the Lecturers' Supplement.

22. £50,000 is invested at 5.5% for 6 years. If all interest is reinvested

    a) What would be the principal at the end of the 6 years?

    b) How much interest would have been received during the 6 years?

23. A car is purchased for £3000 deposit and 5 annual payments of £1000. What is the cost of the car at today's prices if a discount rate of 8% is assumed?

24. A project involves an investment of £2m and is guaranteed to produce an income of £0.5m each year for the next 5 years. Compare and contrast different methods for evaluating the worth of this project. Assume that the income occurs at the end of each year and that the discount rate is 7%.

25. A project costs £5m to set up and a return of £2m p.a for the next three years is guaranteed. A project will only be accepted if the internal rate of return is greater than 14%. Should the project be accepted?

Assignment

MOS plc is a computer software company and its main business is in the development of payroll systems. Recently it has also developed a number of specialised machine control systems and the company is keen to expand into this area. However, the risks in developing these types of systems are much greater than for payroll systems. This is partly to do with the fact that there is a risk that the software will not work but also to do with the fact that it takes much longer for the project to be completed. A payroll system can be developed in under a year while for control systems the development time can be 2 to 3 years. The policy of the company is to lease the software for a fixed period of time and during this period the client pays an annual rental that diminishes with time.

When MOS receives a request for a piece of software, a valuation exercise takes place. This valuation exercise looks at the financial implications as well as any technical problems. For payroll systems the market is very competitive and there is very little room for manoeuvre. However, for control systems there is much more flexibility in pricing. As with any small company, MOS has a limited amount of capital available, which currently amounts to £500,000 obtained through bank loans. MOS currently pays interest at a rate of 8.5% p.a.

MOS has options on three projects. Projects A and B are payroll systems and both involve an expenditure of less than £100,000 while Project C is a specialised control system that involves an expenditure of £500,000. Details of the expenditure and leasing rental is shown in the table below:

Year	Project A (£000's)	Project B (£000's)	Project C (£000's)
0	60	–80	–500
1	30	40	0.0
2	30	20	0.0
3	20	20	0.0
4	10	20	500
5	10	5	300
6			200
7			100

Use investment appraisal techniques to decide which (if any) of the projects should be accepted. Write a note to the M.D of MOS plc explaining your results and recommendations.

3 *Time series analysis*

3.1 *Introduction*

Many variables have values that change with time. For example the weekly sales of ice cream, the monthly unemployment figures and the daily production rates for a factory. The changing value of such variables over a period of time is called a time series. The analysis of time series data is very important, both for industry and government and a large number of people are employed to do this analysis. This chapter will look at the main features of a time series and demonstrate some popular techniques.

On completing this chapter you should be able:

❏ Use the technique of moving averages to isolate the trend in a time series.

❏ Understand the circumstances where the additive and multiplicative models should be used.

❏ Calculate the seasonal component for both the additive and multiplicative models.

❏ Obtain the seasonally adjusted series.

❏ Apply the technique of exponential smoothing in appropriate circumstances.

❏ Use time series analysis to make forecasts.

3.2 *The decomposition model*

This model assumes that a time series is made up of several components. These components are:

❏ Trend

❏ Seasonality

❏ Cyclic behaviour

❏ Randomness

The trend represents the long run behaviour of the data and can be increasing, decreasing or constant. Seasonality relates to periodic fluctuations that repeat themselves at fixed intervals of time. Cyclic behaviour represents the ups and downs of the economy or of a specific industry. It is a long term fluctuation and for practical purposes is usually ignored. Randomness is always present in a time series and represents variation that cannot be explained. Some time series (for example share prices) have a very high random component and the forecasts of these series will be subject to a high degree of error.

Example

Table 1 below consists of data relating to the sales of petrol at the Star petrol station for the past 3 weeks, while table 2 consists of the sales of sun cream by Mace Skin Care plc.

Table 1 Petrol				Table 2 Sun cream		
Week	Day	Litres		Year	Quarter	Sales
1	M	28				(£000's)
	T	16		1991	1	6.00
	W	24			2	9.00
	TH	44			3	12.00
	F	65			4	8.00
	S	82		1992	1	8.00
	SU	30			2	13.50
2	M	33			3	17.00
	T	21			4	13.00
	W	29		1993	1	12.00
	TH	49			2	20.25
	F	70			3	30.00
	S	87			4	19.50
	SU	35		1994	1	18.00
3	M	35				
	T	23				
	W	31				
	TH	51				
	F	72				
	S	89				
	SU	37				

Activity 1

Plot the two series represented by tables 1 and 2 on graph paper and compare and contrast the important features of each.

You can check your graph with the ones in Figures 1 and 2. What can you say about these graphs? You should notice that both series show a marked seasonal component since the pattern repeats themselves at regular intervals. In the case of the Star petrol station, the highest sales always occurs on a Saturday and the lowest on a Monday. The time series for the quarterly sales of a sun cream by Mace Skin Care plc shows a peak in quarter 3 and a trough in quarter 1. You also should notice that the sales of the sun cream appears to have increased rapidly during the three year period.

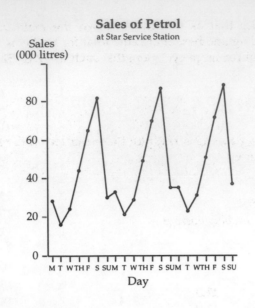

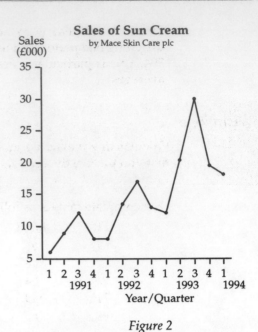

Figure 1 *Figure 2*

3.3 Isolating the trend

To isolate the trend you need to remove the seasonal fluctuations. In the case of the petrol sales the pattern repeats itself every week, so perhaps the average sales each week would be a useful calculation?

Activity 2

Calculate the average petrol sales for weeks 1, 2 and 3. Does this help remove the seasonal fluctuations?

The values you should have got are 41.3, 46.3 and 48.3 for weeks 1, 2 and 3 respectively. The seasonal fluctuations have certainly been removed but then so has most of the data! This is therefore not the best of methods. However, why use Monday to Sunday as a week? Why not Tuesday to Monday or Wednesday to Tuesday? If you think along these lines you will see that many more than three averages can be obtained. This is called *moving averages* since the average is moved by one time period each time. Since there are 7 days or periods in this example you have to calculate a 7-point moving average.

The calculations for the first three averages are shown in the table below. Notice that the first average has been placed alongside Thursday, this is because Thursday is the middle of the week that starts on Monday.

Day	Petrol sales (000's litres)	Weekly total	7-Point Moving average
Monday	28		
Tuesday	16		
Wednesday	24		
Thursday	44	28+16+24+44+65+82+30 = 289	289/7 = 41.3
Friday	65	16+24+44+65+82+30+33 = 294	294/7 = 42.0
Saturday	82	24+44+65+82+30+33+21 = 299	299/7 = 42.7
Sunday	30		
Monday	33		
Tuesday	21		

(Note: A shortcut is to notice that as you move down the table you are simply dropping one period and adding another. That is the total for Friday is 289 – 28 + 33 = 294. This is particularly useful for large cycle lengths, such as 12 or 52 point moving averages)

Activity 3

Calculate the remaining moving averages and plot these figures on the same graph that you plotted the original series.

The complete table is as follows:

Day	Litres	Moving average
M	28	
T	16	
W	24	
TH	44	41.3
F	65	42.0
S	82	42.7
SU	30	43.4
M	33	44.1
T	21	44.9
W	29	45.6
TH	49	46.3
F	70	46.6
S	87	46.9
SU	35	47.1
M	35	47.4
T	23	47.7
W	31	48.0
TH	51	48.3
F	72	
S	89	
SU	37	

The moving average figures have been superimposed on the original time series graph and is shown in Figure 3 below.

There is no doubt that the moving average has smoothed the data and therefore this second series should represent the trend. You can see from the graph that there is a slight upward movement to this trend.

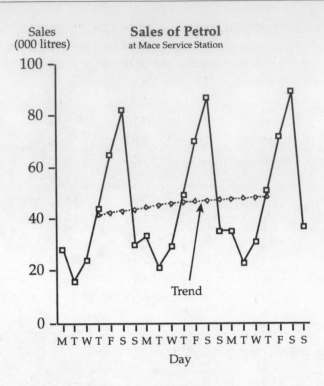

Figure 3

The Star Petrol Station example illustrated the case where the moving average was based on an odd number of periods (seven days). However with the sun cream series there is an even number of periods (four quarters). The problem with this is that the middle of the year falls between quarter two and three. This wouldn't be very helpful since the original data relates to a specific quarter. (How would you plot a value between two quarters and what would this value mean?). To get around this problem, centred moving averages are used. The moving averages are worked out as before, placing the averages between periods. Pairs of averages are then taken and the average of the averages can be written down alongside a specific period. The table below illustrates the calculations.

Year	Quarter	Sales	Moving average	Centred moving average
1991	1	6		
	2	9		
			8.75	
	3	12		(8.75+9.25)/2 = 9.00
			9.25	
	4	8		(9.25+10.38)/2 = 9.81
			10.38	
1992	1	8		
	2	13.5		

Activity 4

Calculate the remaining centred moving average figures for the sales of sun cream and plot these figures on the same graph as you plotted the original series.

You should have obtained the following table.

Year	Quarter	Sales (£000's)	Centred moving average
1991	1	6.00	
	2	9.00	
	3	12.00	9.00
	4	8.00	9.81
1992	1	8.00	11.00
	2	13.50	12.25
	3	17.00	13.38
	4	13.00	14.72
1993	1	12.00	17.19
	2	20.25	19.63
	3	30.00	21.19
	4	19.50	
1994	1	18.00	

The centred moving averages have been plotted on the graph below. Notice the rapidly rising trend values.

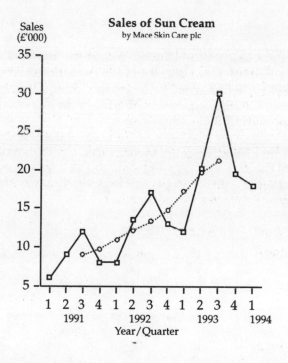

Figure 4

3.4 Isolating the seasonal component

There are two models that will allow you to isolate the seasonal component. The first is the additive model and is applicable if the seasonal swings are a constant difference from the trend. This means that the difference between the trend and a particular period remains approximately constant throughout the entire time series. The second model is the multiplicative model and is applicable if the seasonal swings are a percentage of the trend; that is the seasonal swing will depend on the value of the trend at that point.

31

In equation form the additive model is: $\quad Y = T + S + C + R$

and the multiplicative model is: $\quad\quad Y = T \times S \times C \times R$

Where Y is the variable of interest, T is the trend, S is the seasonal component, C is the cyclic component and R is the random element.

Activity 5

By examining Figure 3 decide whether the additive or multiplicative model is more appropriate for the petrol sales series. Repeat this exercise for the sales of sun cream, using Figure 4.

You should have found that the seasonal swings about the trend for the petrol sales series appear reasonably constant, so an additive model is probably appropriate here. In the sun cream example the seasonal swings about the trend are increasing, so the multiplicative model is probably the better model in this case. However, it is not always so clear cut and sometimes both models are tried and the results compared. To show this, both models will now be applied to the sun cream example.

To obtain the seasonal differences, the additive model can be rearranged as:

$$S + C + R = Y - T$$

So the value of the variable minus the trend value at that point will give you the seasonal difference plus the cyclic and random components. The cyclic component can only be isolated when values of the variable Y are available over many years (at least twenty), which is rare. Usually the cyclic component is ignored and its effect (if any) forms part of the random element.

For quarter 3 of 1990 the estimate of the seasonal difference is $12 - 9 = 3$. This tells you that sales for quarter 3 in 1990 is 3 units (£3000) above the trend. For quarter 4 of 1990 the seasonal difference is -1.81 ($8 - 9.81$), which means the sales are 1.81 below the trend.

Activity 6

Continue this procedure and obtain the seasonal differences for the remainder of the data.

You should have obtained the table shown below:

Year	Quarter	Sales (£000's)	Centred moving average	Seasonal difference
1991	1	6.00		
	2	9.00		
	3	12.00	9.00	3.00
	4	8.00	9.81	−1.81
1992	1	8.00	11.00	−3.00
	2	13.50	12.25	1.25
	3	17.00	13.38	3.63
	4	13.00	14.72	−1.72
1993	1	12.00	17.19	−5.19
	2	20.25	19.63	0.63
	3	30.00	21.19	8.81
	4	19.50		
1994	1	18.00		

If you look at these figures you will notice that for the same quarter number the seasonal difference varies. This is due to the random element. This variation can best be observed in a table similar to the one below, which also allows the average seasonal difference to be calculated.

Quarter	1	2	3	4	
1991			3.00	−1.81	
1992	−3.00	1.25	3.63	−1.72	
1993	−5.19	0.63	8.81		
Average	−4.09	0.94	5.15	−1.77	Sum = 0.22
Adj. Av.	−4.15	0.88	5.09	−1.82	Sum = 0.00

The use of an average value helps to remove some of the random component. These averages should sum to zero since they should cancel out over the year. In the example above you will see that −4.09 + 0.94 + 5.15 − 1.77 = 0.22, which is clearly not zero. If each average is reduced by 0.06 (0.22/4) then you will get the adjusted figures above and you should check that their sum is now zero.

The calculations for the multiplicative model are similar except that S is called the seasonal factor and is worked out by dividing Y by T. These factors are often expressed in percentage form by multiplying by 100.

For example, the seasonal factor for quarter 3 1991 is $\frac{12}{9} \times 100 = 133.3\%$

Activity 7

Obtain the average percentage seasonal factors for the sales of sun cream by Mace Skin Care plc.

The table of seasonal factors that you should have arrived at is shown below.

Year	Quarter	Sales (£000's)	Centred moving average	Seasonal factor (%)
1991	1	6.00		
	2	9.00		
	3	12.00	9.00	133.3
	4	8.00	9.81	81.5
1992	1	8.00	11.00	72.7
	2	13.50	12.25	110.2
	3	17.00	13.38	127.1
	4	13.00	14.72	88.3
1993	1	12.00	17.19	69.8
	2	20.25	19.63	103.2
	3	30.00	21.19	141.6
	4	19.50		
1994	1	18.00		

In this model a seasonal factor above 100% represents sales above the trend and a value below 100% represents sales below the trend. The table below is again used to calculate the adjusted average factors.

Quarter	1	2	3	4	
1991			133.3	81.5	
1992	72.7	110.2	127.1	88.3	
1993	69.8	103.2	141.6		
Average	71.3	106.7	134.0	84.9	Sum = 396.9
Adj. Av.	71.8	107.5	135.1	85.6	Sum = 400.0

Each average was adjusted by multiplying its value by $1.0078 \left(\dfrac{400}{396.9} \right)$, since the sum of the averages should in this case be 400.

3.5 Analysis of errors

Once you have isolated the trend and seasonal components it is a good idea to see how well the model fits the data. This is particularly important when you are not sure whether the additive or multiplicative model is the correct model to use.

For the additive model $Y = T + S$, so the Y variable can be predicted by adding the trend to the relevant adjusted average seasonal difference. For the multiplicative model $Y = T \times S$, so the prediction is made by multiplying the trend and adjusted average seasonal factor. In both cases the difference between the actual value and predicted value gives you the error in the prediction. For example, the predicted sales of sun cream for quarter 3 1991 using the additive model is $9.00 + 5.09 = 14.09$. Since the actual value is 12.00, this represents an error of −2.09 (12 − 14.09).

Using the multiplicative model the predicted value is $9.00 \times \dfrac{135.1}{100} = 12.15$ and the error is now −0.15.

Activity 8

Calculate the remaining errors using both the additive and multiplicative models.

The errors for both models can be seen in the tables below.

Additive model

Year	Qtr	Sales	T	S	Pred Sales	Error
1991	1	6.00				
	2	9.00				
	3	12.00	9.00	5.09	14.09	−2.09
	4	8.00	9.81	−1.80	8.01	0.01
1992	1	8.00	11.00	−4.10	6.90	1.15
	2	13.50	12.25	0.88	13.13	0.37
	3	17.00	13.38	5.09	18.46	−1.46
	4	13.00	14.72	−1.80	12.90	0.10
1993	1	12.00	17.19	−4.10	13.04	−1.04
	2	20.25	19.63	0.88	20.51	−0.26
	3	30.00	21.19	5.09	26.28	3.72
	4	19.50				
1994	1	18.00				

Multiplicative model

Year	Qtr	Sales	T	S	Pred Sales	Error
1991	1	6.00				
	2	9.00				
	3	12.00	9.00	135.1	12.15	−0.15
	4	8.00	9.81	85.6	8.40	−0.40
1992	1	8.00	11.00	71.8	7.90	0.10
	2	13.50	12.25	107.5	13.17	0.33
	3	17.00	13.38	135.1	18.06	−1.06
	4	13.00	14.72	85.6	12.60	0.40
1993	1	12.00	17.19	71.8	12.35	−0.35
	2	20.25	19.63	107.5	21.10	−0.85
	3	30.00	21.19	135.1	28.63	1.37
	4	19.50				
1994	1	18.00				

The errors should be small and show no pattern. Even with small quantities of data the easiest way to look at the errors is by means of a graph. Figures 5 and 6, below show that the multiplicative model gives the smallest errors and is therefore the better model, which is what was expected.

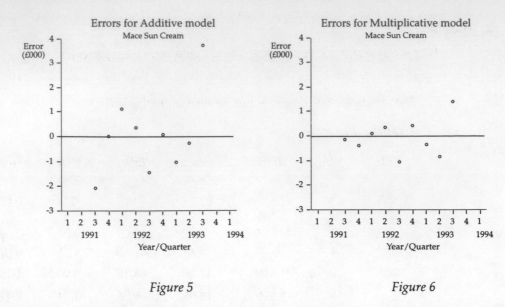

Figure 5   Figure 6

Apart from a graphical display of the errors, it is possible to analyse them statistically. Two statistics are normally calculated, the mean absolute deviation (MAD) and the mean square deviation (MSE). The formulae for these are:

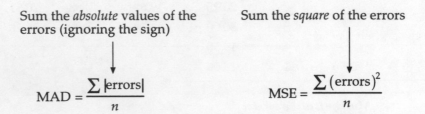

Sum the *absolute* values of the errors (ignoring the sign)

Sum the *square* of the errors

$$MAD = \frac{\sum |errors|}{n}$$

$$MSE = \frac{\sum (errors)^2}{n}$$

The MAD statistic is simply the mean of the absolute errors (or deviations), while MSE is the mean of the square deviations. Both statistics are valid but you will find that many statisticians favour the MSE statistic. One reason for this is that squaring puts more emphasis on large errors. For the sun cream example the calculation of MAD and MSE using the errors obtained from the additive model is as follows:

Additive model

Year	Qtr	Actual Sales	Predicted Sales	Error	Absolute error	Squared error
1991	3	12.00	14.09	−2.09	2.09	4.3681
	4	8.00	7.99	0.01	0.01	0.0001
1992	1	8.00	6.85	1.15	1.15	1.3225
	2	13.50	13.13	0.37	0.37	0.1369
	3	17.00	18.46	−1.46	1.46	2.1316
	4	13.00	12.90	0.10	0.10	0.0100
1993	1	12.00	13.04	−1.04	1.04	1.0816
	2	20.25	20.51	−0.26	0.26	0.0676
	3	30.00	26.28	3.72	3.72	13.8380
				Sum =	10.20	22.9564
				Mean =	1.13	2.55

Activity 9

Repeat the above calculation using the multiplicative model.

You should have obtained the following table.

Multiplicative model

Year	Qtr	Actual Sales	Predicted Sales	Error	Absolute error	Squared error
1991	3	12.00	12.15	–0.15	0.15	0.0225
	4	8.00	8.40	–0.40	0.40	0.1600
1992	1	8.00	7.90	0.10	0.10	0.0100
	2	13.50	13.17	0.33	0.33	0.1089
	3	17.00	18.06	–1.06	1.06	1.1236
	4	13.00	12.60	0.40	0.40	0.1600
1993	1	12.00	12.35	–0.35	0.35	0.1225
	2	20.25	21.10	–0.85	0.85	0.7225
	3	30.00	28.63	1.37	1.37	1.8769
				Sum =	5.01	4.3069
				Mean =	0.56	0.48

Both these statistics are smaller than that obtained with the additive model, demonstrating once again that the multiplicative model is better for this example.

3.6 Seasonally adjusted series

I am sure that you have heard the phrase 'seasonally adjusted' when economic time series are mentioned by the media. A common example is unemployment. If a series is seasonally adjusted it means that the seasonal component has been removed, leaving the trend component. By seasonally adjusting unemployment figures, for example, it is easy to tell what is happening to this important economic variable.

For the additive model a time series is seasonally adjusted by *subtracting* the seasonal difference, while for the multiplicative model the operation is one of *division*.

Normally this procedure is used when new data arrives and you want to see if there is any change in the trend of the series. For example, say that the petrol sales at Star petrol station for the Monday of the fourth week is 38,000 litres. This value can be seasonally adjusted by subtracting –4.15 (the average seasonal difference for Mondays). Since this value is negative the net result is to add 4.15 to 38, which is 42.15 or 42,150 litres.

The average seasonal factor for quarter 2 is 107.5% (see page 34) so the seasonally

adjusted sales is $\dfrac{28500}{1.075} = £26,512$.

3.7 Forecasting using the decomposition model

One purpose of time series analysis is to use the results to forecast future values of the series. The procedure for this is to extrapolate the trend into the future and then apply the seasonal component to the forecast trend. There are various methods of extrapolating the trend. If the trend is approximately linear then linear regression could be used by assigning numerical values to time. For example, using the sun cream series quarter 1 1991 would have a value 1 and quarter 1 1994 would have a value 13). However, you will often find it easier to extrapolate by eye ('eyeballing') since other factors can then be considered, if necessary. If there is doubt about the future behaviour of the trend, you could make two or three different extrapolations to give different forecasts (say an optimistic and a pessimistic one).

For the sun cream example, a possible extrapolation of the trend has been made and can be seen in Figure 7 below. The forecast trend values for the remainder of 1993 have been read off this graph and are shown below:

Quarter	2	3	4
Trend forecast	25.5	27.0	28.5

To calculate the forecast for each quarter using the multiplicative model these trend forecasts need to be multiplied by the appropriate seasonal factor. For example, for quarter 2 the average seasonal factor is 107.5% so the forecasted value is:

$$25.5 \times 1.075 = 27.41 \text{ or } £27,400 \text{ approximately}$$

For the additive model the average seasonal difference of 0.88 is added to 25.5, that is 26.38 or about £26,400. The result using the multiplicative model is likely to be more accurate since the model had smaller errors. However, any forecasts are subject to considerable uncertainty and all forecasts should be treated with caution.

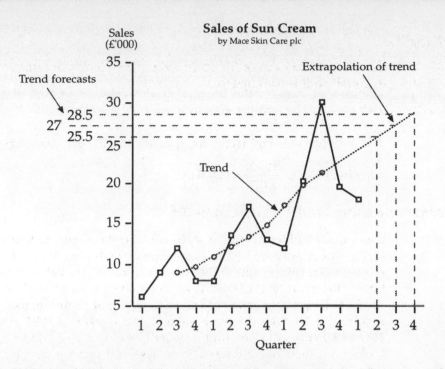

Figure 7

Activity 11

Use the multiplicative model to obtain forecasts for quarters 3 and 4 of 1994.

The seasonal factors for quarter 3 and 4 are 135.1% and 85.6% so the forecasts will be:

$$27 \times 1.351 = \quad 36.477 \quad \text{(£36,500 approximately)}$$
$$\text{and} \quad 28.5 \times 0.856 = \quad 24.396 \quad \text{(£24,400 approximately)}$$

3.8 Exponential smoothing

The technique of exponential smoothing is often used where a short term forecast is required (that is the next period). The formula for this technique is very simple. It is:

$$\text{Next forecast} = \text{Last forecast} + \alpha \times \text{error in last forecast}$$

Where α (alpha) is a smoothing constant. This constant takes a value between 0 and 1 so that the next forecast will simply be the last forecast plus a fraction of the last error. The error in the last forecast is the actual value minus the forecast.

To illustrate this technique imagine that you are responsible for ensuring that the Small Brewery company has sufficient barrels available to store its beer. Full barrels are sent out and empty ones returned. You need to know how many barrels will be returned the next day to plan production. If insufficient barrels are available, beer is wasted whereas if more barrels than expected are returned you may have lost sales.

There are two problems with exponential smoothing. The first is what value of alpha to use. This can only be found by trial and error and you may even have to change the value in the light of experience. It is usually found that a value between 0.05 and 0.3 gives the smallest values of MAD or MSE. For the Small Brewery company, a value of 0.1 has been chosen.

The second problem is how to get the first forecast since a last forecast is required. Some people choose a suitable value while others prefer a warm up period. Once several forecasts have been made the starting value becomes less important anyway, but let us suppose that you have decided to use the warm up method. You are to use the last ten days for this purpose and therefore your first proper forecast will be for day eleven. The number of barrels returned over the last ten days are:

Day	1	2	3	4	5	6	7	8	9	10
No of barrels	20	13	19	19	25	17	15	13	22	20

If you take the forecast for day two as the actual for day one then the error is -7 $(13 - 20)$ and the forecast for day three becomes:

$$20 + (0.1 \times -7) = 19.3$$

The forecast for day four is now:

$$19.3 + (0.1 \times -0.3) = 19.27$$

and so on ...

Activity 12

Continue this process to achieve a forecast for day 11.

You will probably find it easier if you use a table similar to the one below:

Day	No. barrels	Forecast	Error	$\alpha \times error$	Next forecast
1	20				
2	13	20.00	-7.00	-0.70	19.30
3	19	19.30	-0.30	-0.03	19.27
4	19	19.27	-0.27	-0.03	19.24
5	25	19.24	5.76	0.58	19.82
6	17	19.82	-2.82	-0.28	19.54
7	15	19.54	-4.54	-0.45	19.08
8	13	19.08	-6.08	-0.61	18.47
9	22	18.47	3.53	0.35	18.83
10	20	18.83	1.17	0.12	18.94
11		18.94			

As you can see the forecast for day eleven is 18.94 (that is 19 barrels).

The time series of the original data and of the forecast values is shown in Figure 8 below. Also shown is the forecast using $\alpha = 0.5$ and you will see that a value of 0.1 gives a smoother series. This is generally true, the smaller the value of α the greater the smoothing effect.

In terms of accuracy the errors can again be analysed and MAD and MSE calculated (See page 36). Using $\alpha = 0.1$, an MSE of 17.96 is obtained.

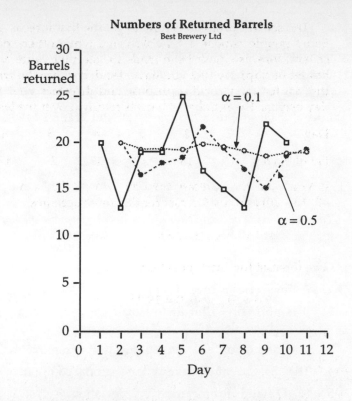

Numbers of Returned Barrels
Best Brewery Ltd

Figure 8

Activity 13

Calculate the MSE statistic using an alpha of 0.5

By using an alpha of 0.5 you should have found that the MSE statistics has increased to 23.21.

Simple exponential smoothing is a very useful and easy to use short term forecasting technique. However it will lag behind a series that is undergoing a sharp change such as a series that has a seasonal component or a steep trend.

3.9 Summary

A time series can contain a seasonal component, a trend and some randomness. The trend in the series can be observed by using the technique of moving averages, while the seasonal component can be isolated by the use of an appropriate decomposition model. The additive decomposition model is used when the seasonal swings are approximately constant while the multiplicative model is more appropriate when the seasonal swings are a proportion of the trend. The errors in the models can be observed by the use of suitable graphs or error statistics can be calculated. Future values of a time series can be seasonally adjusted by either subtracting the seasonal difference from the new data (additive model) or by dividing the new data by the seasonal factor. Finally future values of a time series can be predicted by extrapolating the trend. This is best done 'by eye' although linear regression can be used if the trend is linear.

This chapter also introduced exponential smoothing, which is an excellent short term forecasting method.

3.10 Further reading

Morris, C, *Quantitative Approaches in Business Studies*, Pitman, 1993, Chapter 14

Harper, W, *Statistics, M & E Handbook Series*, Pitman, 1991, Chapter 15.

Oakshott, L, *Quantitative Approaches to Decision Making*, DP Publications, 1993, Unit 14.

Lucey, T, *Quantitative Techniques*, DP Publications, 1992, Chapter 9.

3.11 Exercises

Progress questions

These question have been designed to help you remember the key points in this chapter. The answers to these questions are given in Appendix 1, page 108.

Give the missing word in each case:

1. A time series is made up of a trend, seasonality, cyclic component and ....

2. It is normally difficult to isolate the .... component unless a very long time series is available.

3. The method of .... averages is used to remove the seasonal fluctuations.

4. The .... model allows the seasonal component to be isolated.

5. MAD stands for mean .... deviation.

Answer TRUE or FALSE

6. If the seasonal swings are increasing it is likely that the multiplicative model will be more accurate than the additive model.

    True ☐ False ☐

7. For a 12-point moving average it is necessary to centre the moving averages.

    True ☐ False ☐

8. To seasonal adjust a time series you multiply by the seasonal factor.

    True ☐ False ☐

9. Exponential smoothing is a short term forecasting technique.

    True ☐ False ☐

Review questions

These questions have been designed to help you check your comprehension of the key points in this chapter. You may wish to look further than this chapter in order to answer them fully. You will find the reading list useful in this respect. You can check the essential elements of your answers by refer-ring to the appropriate section.

10. What is the purpose of moving averages? (Section 3.2)

11. Describe the essential differences between the additive and multiplicative models. (Section 3.4)

12. How can you measure the accuracy of a time series model? (Section 3.5)

Multiple choice questions

The answers to these will be given in the Lecturers' Supplement.

13. A time series is made up of monthly data. The moving average is likely to be calculated using:
    A   A 5-point moving average
    B   A 10-point moving average
    C   A 12-point moving average

14. The sum of additive seasonal differences should be:
    A   0
    B   1
    C   depends on the data

15. Exponential smoothing allows a forecast for:
    A   The next time period
    B   The next two time periods
    C   A full cycle ahead

16. Three of the seasonal factors for a time series based on a quarterly cycle are 89%, 130%, and 75%. The fourth factor is:
    A   94%
    B   106%
    C   100%

17. The seasonal difference for period 1 of a time series is 25.5. The next period 1 has a value of 185. The seasonally adjusted value for the this period is:
    A   159.5
    B   210.5
    C   47.175

18. The errors using a particular time series are: 2.5, –3.6, 5.8, 10.1, –6.3, –2.2, 10.2, –15.0, 0.3, –1.8. The MAD statistic for this data is:
    A   57.8
    B   5.78
    C   0.578

19.   The MSE statistic using the errors in question 18. is:
    A   53.176
    B   5.3176
    C   531.76

Practice questions

Answers to these questions will be given in the Lecturers' Supplement.

20. You have just completed an analysis into the sales of a computer game over the past 3 years and the result is shown as follows.

Year	Period	Sales (000's)
1991	1	30
	2	35
	3	35
	4	40
	5	50
	6	60
1992	1	30
	2	40
	3	38
	4	35
	5	52
	6	60
1993	1	35
	2	33
	3	37
	4	43
	5	50
	6	65

a) Plot this series on graph paper.

b) From the raw data, calculate the moving average series and plot this on the graph. Comment on both series of data.

c) Use the additive decomposition model to obtain average seasonal differences for each period.

d) Obtain rough forecasts for 1994

21. The personnel department of BBS plc, a large food processing company, is concerned about absenteeism among its shop floor workforce. There is a general feeling that the underlying trend has been rising, but nobody has yet analysed the figures. The total number of shop-floor employees has remained virtually unchanged over the last few years.

The mean number of absentees per day is given below for each quarter of the years 1991 to 1993 and quarter 1 of 1994.

	Q1	Q2	Q3	Q4
1991	25.1	14.4	9.5	23.7
1992	27.9	16.9	12.4	26.1
1993	31.4	19.7	15.9	29.9
1994	34.5			

a) Plot the above data on a graph (leave space for the remaining 1994 figures).

b) Use the method of moving averages to determine the trend in the series and superimpose this on your graph. Interpret your graph.

c) Use an appropriate method to measure the seasonal pattern in the data. Briefly give reasons for your choice of method.

d) Use your analysis to produce rough forecasts of the mean number of absentees there will be in the remaining quarters of 1994.

22. The following data refers to the end of business share prices for a particular company:

112, 111, 113, 115, 114, 112, 115, 111, 111, 112, 113

Use exponential smoothing with a smoothing constant of 0.1 to forecast the price on day 12.

Assignment

Answers to this assignment will be given in the Lecturers' Supplement.

Use statistical publications in the library (for example, the Monthly Digest of Statistics) to obtain a time series of your choice. Carry out a full analysis of this series.

Write a report of your analysis including tables and graphs. Provide justification for the model used including graphs of errors and error statistics. Use you model to provide appropriate forecasts.

4 *Linear programming*

4.1 *Introduction*

Industry and business in general operate with limited resources. Money, material and space is frequently scarce and companies attempt to utilise these scarce resources as efficiently as is possible. The technique of linear programming is a procedure that can provide the best solution to many problems that involve an objective, such as profit maximisation and a series of (linear) constraints, such as time, labour and cost. This chapter introduces this technique and applies it to simple problems that can be solved graphically.

On completing this chapter you should be able to:

❑ Formulate linear programming problems for both maximising and minimising problems.

❑ Use a graphical method to solve two variable problems

❑ Understand the concept of shadow prices and be able to calculate their value

❑ Carry out a sensitivity analysis on the problem

4.2 *Basics of linear programming*

Linear programming (or L.P for short) is concerned with the management of scarce resources. It is particularly applicable where two or more activities are competing for these limited resources. For example, a company might want to make several different products but each product makes different demands on the limited resources available. How many of each product should be made so that contribution to profits is maximised? Or perhaps you want to determine the quantities of ingredients necessary for a particular blend of food that will minimise the cost of production.

Before these and other problems can be solved you have to formulate the problem in linear programming terms. This involves expressing the problem as a series of inequations and finding solutions to these inequations that optimises some objective. This may sound very difficult but for two variable problems (for example, two products) the problem can be solved using a graphical technique. For larger problems the 'SIMPLEX' algorithm is used, usually by computer

Linear programming requires a knowledge of elementary algebra and the drawing of straight lines. If you are a little rusty in these areas you are advised to work through activities 1 to 5. Otherwise, you can move onto section 4.3, page 50.

Activity 1

Which of the following equations represent straight lines?

    (a) $Y = 2X + 5$ (b) $Y + 4X = 20$ (c) $Y = 8$

    (d) $Y = X$ (e) $Y = X^2$

The equation of a straight line is $Y = mX + c$, where 'm' is the gradient and 'c' is the value of Y when $X = 0$ (often referred to as the 'intercept' on the Y-axis).

Equation (a) is obviously a straight line with $m = 2$ and $c = 5$.

Equation (b) is also a straight line and this may be easier to see if you subtract $4X$ from both sides of the equation.

That is: $\qquad Y = 20 - 4X$

or $\qquad Y = -4X + 20$

This equation is now in the standard form and you should see that $m = -4$ and $c = 20$.

Equation (c) is another straight line but this is a special one. This could be written as

$$Y = 0X + 8$$

and you will see that $m = 0$, that is the gradient is zero. This can be therefore be represented as a horizontal line.

Equation (d) can be written as $Y = X + 0$, so this represents a straight line with a gradient of 1 and 'c' of 0. This line passes through the origin of the graph (that is, $X = 0, Y = 0$).

Equation (e) is not a straight line since Y increases as the square of X. The graphs of these equations are shown in Figure 1, below.

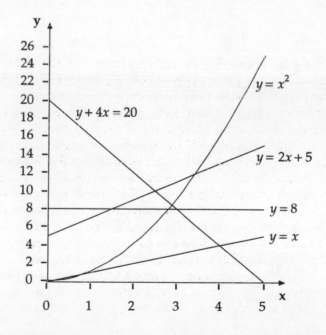

Figure 1

Activity 2

Plot the equations $2Y + X = 8$ and $Y + 2X = 7$ on the same graph and write down the coordinates of the point of intersection.

You should have obtained the graph shown in Figure 2 below. The point of intersection of the two lines is at the point $X = 2$, $Y = 3$. This can be written as $(2,3)$. In this example the coordinates of the point of intersection were both whole numbers, which made it easy to read from your graph. Unfortunately this is not always the case and accurately reading fractional values from a graph is difficult. A better method is the algebraic method of *simultaneous equations*.

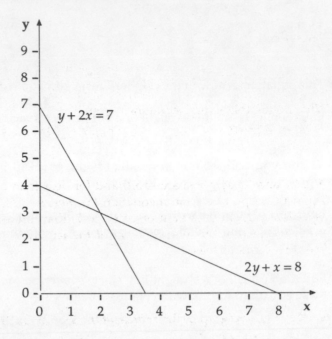

Figure 2

Activity 3

Solve the equations given in Activity 2 simultaneously.

Hopefully your answer agreed with the graphical method. The method I prefer is the method of elimination. To use this method the two equations are written down as follows:

$$Y + 2X = 7 \quad (1)$$

$$2Y + X = 8 \quad (2)$$

The coefficients of either 'X' or 'Y' must be equal in the two equations and this is achieved by multiplying both sides of equation (1) by 2. The equations can now be subtracted:

$$2Y + 4X = 14$$

$$2Y + X = 8$$

$$3X = 6 \quad (Y \text{ has now been 'eliminated'})$$

That is: $\quad X = 2$

This value of 'X' can now be substituted back into either equation (1) or (2) to give the value of 'Y'.

Using equation (2):

$$2Y + 2 = 8$$

$$2Y = 6$$

Therefore $\quad Y = 3$

Activity 4

What do the following inequations mean?

a) $Y + 2x \leq 7$ b) $2Y + X \geq 8$

The '$\leq$' and '$\geq$' symbols are shorthand for 'less than or equal to' and 'greater than or equal to' respectively. So inequation (a) means the sum of the left hand side of the equation must be less than or equal to 7, that is the sum cannot be greater than 7. Inequation (b) means that the sum of the left hand side of the equation must be at least 8; it cannot be less.

Activity 5

How would you graphically represent the two inequations

$$Y + 2X \leq 7$$

and: $2Y + X \geq 8$

And what does the term 'intersection' mean in this case?

Whereas an equation can be represented by a straight line, an inequation is represented by a region. The equation $Y + 2X = 7$ forms the boundary of the region represented by the inequation $Y + 2X \leq 7$. Similarly the equation $2Y + X = 8$ forms the boundary of the region $2Y + X \geq 8$. The region can only be on one side of the boundary and this can be found by inspection; that is a point is investigated to see if it satisfies the inequation. The easiest point to try is the origin ($X = 0$, $Y = 0$), except when the boundary passes through this point. When the region has been found it needs to be identified. This can be done by shading. The normal convention is to shade the unwanted region and this is the convention adopted in this book. You can see this in Figure 3 below.

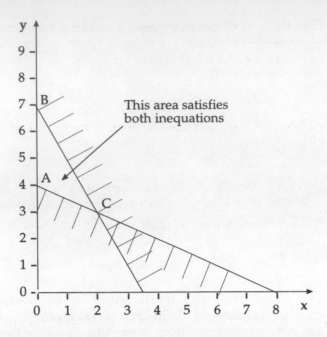

Figure 3

The intersection of regions is the area on the graph that satisfies all inequations. In this example, the area is represented by ABC. Any point within this area (including the boundaries) satisfies both inequations.

4.3 Model formulation

Before a problem can be solved by the L.P method a model needs to developed. The model consists of a description of the problem in mathematical terms. In particular the variables of the problem need to be defined and the objective decided. In addition the constraints need to be expressed as inequations.

The next few activities will take you through the procedure using the following example:

Example 1

The company Just Shirts has been formed to make high quality shirts and is planning to make two types – the 'Regular Fit' and the 'Deluxe Fit'. The contribution to profits for each shirt is £5 for each Regular Fit shirt made and £8 for each Deluxe Fit shirt. To make each shirt requires cotton, of which 600 square metres is available each day and machinists to cut and stitch the shirts. Twenty machinists are employed by the company and they each work an 8 hour day; giving 160 hours of labour in total. Each Regular Fit shirt requires 5 square metre of cotton and takes 1 hour to make, while each Deluxe Fit shirt takes 6 square metres of cotton and 2 hours to make. The company wishes to maximises contribution to profits so how many of each type of shirt should be made on a daily basis?

Activity 6

Define the variables for this problem.

You are required to determine the number of each type of shirts to produce. Some authors suggest using X and Y to represent the variables but I think it is more 'user friendly' to use letters that mean something. I would therefore suggest that you use R to represent the number of Regular Fit shirts that are to be made each day and D to represent the number of Deluxe Fit shirts.

Activity 7

It is required to maximise contribution to profits. How would you express this in equation form?

If you made just one of each type of shirt you would make a profit of £5 + £8. However, you are making R Regular Fit and D Deluxe Fit shirts so the total profit will be $5R + 8D$. This can be written as:

$$\text{Max.} \quad 5R + 8D$$

Activity 8

There is a limit of 600 square metres of cotton available each day. How would you express this as a constraint to production given that each Regular Fit shirt requires 5 square metres and each Deluxe Fit shirt requires 6 square metres?

If you make R Regular Fit shirts then you will use 5R metres of cotton. Similarly you will use 6D metres of cotton to make D Deluxe Fit shirts. The sum of these two must be less than or equal to 600 square metres so this can be written as:

$$5R + 6D \leq 600$$

Activity 9

Repeat Activity 8 for the labour resource.

You will use R hours for the Regular Fit shirt and $2D$ hours for the Deluxe Fit shirt and 160 hours are available each day, so the constraint can be written as:

$$R + 2D \leq 160$$

You have now formulated the problem, although you should indicate that you are only interested in positive values of R and D and the two constraints $R \geq 0$ and $D \geq 0$ will do this for you.

To summarise, the LP formulation for this problem is:

Max: $5R + 8D$

subject to

$$5R + 6D \leq 600$$

$$R + 2D \leq 160$$

$$R, D \geq 0$$

There are many values of R and D that will satisfy these inequations. For instance, $R = 40$ and $D = 20$ would satisfy all the constraints so this is feasible combination. The problem is which combination will give the largest profit?

4.4 Graphical solution of linear programming problems

The formulation of the problem is only the start (but for many students the hardest part). You now have to solve the problem. There are many computer packages on the market that will solve L.P problems but for two variable problems it is possible to solve the problem graphically.

If for the moment you replace the inequality signs by equalities, the two main constraints become:

$$5R + 6D = 600 \quad \text{(cotton)}$$

and $\quad R + 2D = 160 \quad \text{(labour)}$

Since these equations contain only two variables, R and D, they can be represented as straight lines and plotted on a graph. Two points are required to plot a straight line and it is convenient to find where they cross the axes. To do this it is simply a matter of letting $R = 0$ and calculating D and then letting $D = 0$ and calculating R.

Activity 10

Plot the two equations, $R + 2D = 160$ and $5R + 6D = 600$ on graph paper.

The points where the two lines cross the axes are summarised below:

Constraint	R	D
Cotton	0	100
	120	0
Labour	0	80
	160	0

These two lines have been plotted on a graph (see Figure 4) and they mark the boundaries of the inequations. The region satisfying each inequation will be one side of the boundary. In this example the regions for both inequations are below the lines. To identify the required region it is normal to shade the unwanted region, that is the region not satisfying the inequality. The region that satisfies all inequalities is called the feasible region and any point within this region will satisfy all the constraints. The graph for the Just Shirts example is shown in Figure 4 below and you should be able to identify the feasible region as OABC.

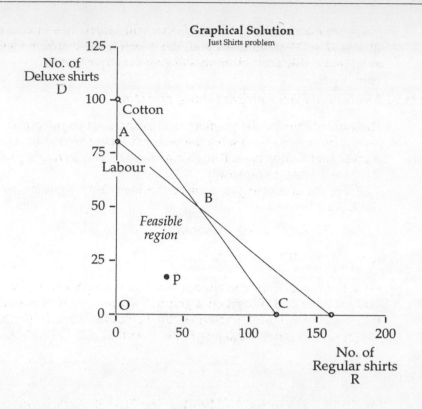

Graphical Solution
Just Shirts problem

Figure 4

Any point within the feasible region will satisfy all constraints but which point or points give the largest profit? Fortunately this can be found quite easily.

4.5 Finding the optimum – the isoprofit/cost method

The point 'p' in Figure 4 is in the feasible region and the profit for this combination is:

$$5 \times 40 + 8 \times 20 = £360$$

However there are other combinations of R and D that give the value of 360 since:

$$5R + 8D = 360$$

Thus the profit equation is just another straight line and can be plotted in the same way as the constraints.

That is if $R = 0$, then $D = 45$ and if $D = 0$ then $R = 72$

This line obviously passes through the point 'p' (see Figure 5, below). Can this figure of 360 be increased? If you try say a value of 500 so that $5R + 6D = 500$ you will get another straight line that is parallel to the first one. The reason for this is that the gradient of the line stays the same – it is only the intercept on the axes that change. This line is called the isoprofit line ('iso' means same).

Activity 11

Place a ruler on the isoprofit line and very carefully move it away from the origin and parallel to the line. What is happening to the profit as the isoprofit line moves away from the origin? At what point does it leave the feasible region completely?

You should have found that as the line moves away from the origin the profit increases and you will find that the point B is the point that is furthest away from the origin, yet still within the feasible region. The fact that the optimum point is at a corner point of the feasible region is no fluke – *the optimum value will always be found at a corner point of the feasible region.*

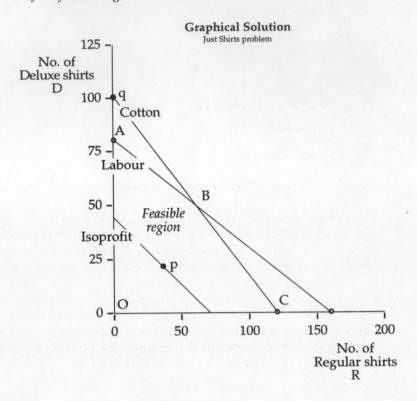

Graphical Solution
Just Shirts problem

Figure 5

The values of R and D at point B can be read off the graph above. You should find that R = 60 and D = 50 and this gives a profit of:

$$5 \times 60 + 8 \times 50 = £700$$

You may find it surprising that at the optimum solution more Regular Fit shirts are made than Deluxe Fit ones – this is because the Deluxe version uses proportionately more resources.

You found the value of R and D from the graph but for greater accuracy it is recommended that the relevant equations are solved algebraically. This is particularly important when the graph shows that fractional values are involved or when it is difficult to decide which point is optimal. The method of simultaneous equations is used to solve for R and D and is as follows:

$$R + 2D = 160 \qquad \text{equation (1)}$$
$$5R + 6D = 600 \qquad \text{equation (2)}$$

multiply (1) by 5 and subtract (1) from (2)

$$5R + 10D = 800$$
$$5R + 6D = 600$$

Thus: $\qquad 4D = 200$

so: $\qquad D = 50$

If $D = 50$ is now substituted back into (1)

$$R + 100 = 160$$
$$R = 60$$

which is the solution found from the graph.

A word of warning. Even if you use simultaneous equations to solve for the two variables you must still draw the graph first. Without drawing the graph you could quite easily solve pairs of equations outside the feasible region. Also the optimum point could be on either axis (for example point A or C in the graph above).

4.6 Finding the optimum – an alternative method

Since you now know that the optimum point must be at a corner point of the feasible region, you could work out the value of the two variables at every such point. For example, at point A the value of R is zero and D is 80, so the profit must be $8 \times 80 = £640$.

Activity 12

Calculate the profit at each of the other corner points.

The profit for each corner point is as follows:

	R	D	Profit
Point A	0	80	£640
Point B	60	50	£700
Point C	120	0	£600

These figures confirm that point B gives the greatest profit.

For feasible regions that have few corner points, this method is probably the quickest. However, it is necessary for you to understand the idea of isoprofit lines as this concept is important when looking at sensitivity analysis.

4.7 Tight and slack constraints

If you substitute the optimal values of R (60) and D (50) back into the constraints you will get the following:

Labour: $60 + 2 \times 50 = 160$

Cotton: $5 \times 60 + 6 \times 50 = 600$

Since these values correspond to the maximum quantity of both resources available, the resources are scarce and are called tight constraints. Where a constraint has not reached its limit it is referred to as a slack constraint. For example, if it was not possible to make more than 70 Deluxe Fit shirts, the constraint would be written as $D \leq 70$. This constraint would be slack because the optimal solution has not reached this limit.

4.8 Sensitivity analysis

Linear programming is a deterministic model, that is, all variables are assumed to be known with certainty. So the quantity of cotton available each day was assumed to be exactly 600 square metres and the contribution to profits of the Regular Fit shirt was assumed to be exactly £5. Of course in reality you will never be 100% certain about the value of many of the parameters in a L.P model and the purpose of sensitivity analysis is to ask 'what-if' type questions about these parameters. For example, what if more cotton can be purchased, or what if the profit of a Regular Fit shirt increased to £6.

Sensitivity analysis in linear programming is concerned with the change in the right hand side of the constraints (normally the resources) and changes to the objective function coefficients (that is the profit/costs of each variable).

4.8.1 Changes to the right hand side of a constraint

Both the labour and cotton resource are tight constraints and an increase in either of these resources will increase the profit made. The reason for this is that as the right hand side of a tight constraint increases, the constraint and the optimum point move away from the origin.

This can be demonstrated by re-solving the simultaneous equations with the right hand side of the labour constraint increased by one to 161. That is:

$R + 2D = 161$

$5R + 6D = 600$

solving these two equations simultaneous as before gives

$$R = 58.5 \text{ and } D = 51.25$$

(don't worry about the fractional values for the time being) and the new profit will be £702.5, an increase of £2.50. This £2.50 is called the shadow price of the labour resource. It is defined as the change in the value of the objective function if the right hand side is increased (or decreased) by one unit.

Activity 13

Calculate the shadow price of the cotton resource.

You should have found that the shadow price of the cotton resource is £0.50 per square metre. That is, an additional profit of 50p could be made for each extra square metre of cotton that could be obtained.

So if it was possible to increase labour hours (perhaps by working overtime) or to increase the supply of cotton, a potentially larger profit could be made. However this assumes that the direct costs do not increase. If for instance overtime rates increase costs by more than £2.50 per hour, then it wouldn't be economic to increase production in this way. However, assuming it is worthwhile, how many more hours should be worked? As the labour constraint moves away from the origin there comes a point where it moves outside the cotton constraint, this is at point 'q' in Figure 5. This means that the labour resource ceases to be scarce and further increase of this resource will just add to the surplus of labour. At point q, $R = 0$ and $D = 100$, so if these values are substituted into the labour equation you will get:

$$0 + 2 \times 100 = 200$$

So the labour resource can increase by 40 hours (200 − 160), which means a possible $40 \times 2.50 = £100$ extra profit can be made each day.

Activity 14

What additional quantity of cotton would it be worth purchasing and what additional profit would result?

You should have found that the supply of cotton can be increased to 800 square metres per day, which is an additional 200 square metres. The extra profit would be £100.

4.8.2 Changes to the objective function coefficients

The objective function for the Just Shirts example is:

$$\text{Max. } 5R + 8D$$

Where 5 (in £) is the contribution to profits for each Regular Fit shirt made and 8 is the profit per Deluxe Fit shirt. If it was possible to reduce costs then profits per shirt would rise and vice versa, but would the production of 60 Regular Fit shirts and 50 Deluxe Fit shirts remain the optimal solution?

Activity 15

Assume that the profit on a Regular Fit shirt has decreased to £2. Re-draw the isoprofit line to see if the optimum point has changed.

Figure 6, below shows the effect on the isoprofit line of reducing the profit of a Regular Fit shirt to £2.

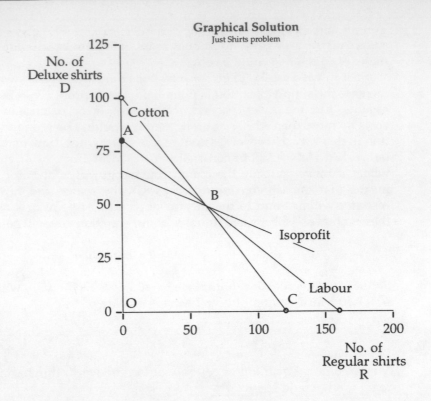

Graphical Solution
Just Shirts problem

Figure 6

The optimum solution has changed and is now at point A. In this solution you would make 80 Deluxe Fit shirts but no Regular Fit ones.

Although you could find the optimum point each time a change in the profit coefficient was made, it would be much easier if you knew the value of the profit that would cause a change in the optimal solution. If you let the profit be 'P' the isoprofit line has the equation:

$$P = 5R + 8D$$

Re-arranging this equation into the form $Y = mX + c$ gives:

$$D = -\frac{5}{8}R + \frac{P}{8}$$

The gradient of this line is $-\frac{5}{8}$.

This gradient is simply the profit on a Regular Fit shirt divided by the profit of a Deluxe Fit shirt. If the profit on the Regular Fit shirt is £2 then the gradient of the isoprofit line becomes $-\frac{5}{8}$.

Now consider what happens as the isoprofit line changes from a gradient of $-\frac{5}{8}$ to $-\frac{2}{8}$.

At some point it must become parallel to the labour constraint line and at this point the same profit will be obtained at both points A and B. (In fact all points along the line AB would give the same profit – this is known as multiple optimal solutions).

To find the profit of the Regular Fit shirt that would make the isoprofit line parallel to the labour constraint, you need to work out the gradient of this line. Rearranging the equation R + 2D = 160 into the standard $Y = MX + C$ form will give you

$$2D = 160 - R$$

that is

$$D = 80 - \frac{1}{2}R$$

or

$$D = -\frac{1}{2}R + 80$$

The gradient is therefore $-\frac{1}{2}$.

You now need to find the value of the profit on a Regular Fit shirt that will give you this gradient. This can be done with the help of some elementary algebra:

Let x be the unknown value of the profit, then the gradient of the isoprofit line is $-\frac{x}{8}$ and:

$$-\frac{x}{8} = -\frac{1}{2}$$

This gives $x = 4$, so if the profit of a Regular Fit shirt falls below £4 the optimum solution changes to point A on the graph ($R = 0$ and $D = 80$). This is the lower limit for the profit of the Regular Fit shirt. There is also an upper limit and you are advised to tackle the next activity.

Activity 16

Using the same procedure as above, calculate the *upper* value of the Regular Fit profit.

The upper limit can be found when the isoprofit line becomes parallel to BC and since the gradient of the cotton line is $-\frac{5}{6}$ the equation becomes:

$$-\frac{x}{8} = -\frac{5}{6}$$

This gives $x = 6.67$, so if the profit of a Regular Fit shirt rises above £6.67 the optimum solution changes to point C on the graph ($R = 120$ and $D = 0$).

Activity 17

Calculate the range of the profit of the Deluxe Fit shirt within which the optimal solution stays the same.

This again requires you to find the lower and upper values of the profit. You should have found that this profit range is from £6 to £10.

4.9 Minimisation problems

The Just Shirts example was a maximisation problem because a solution was required that maximised the contribution to profits. However, equally important are minimisation problems in which some objective, for example cost, is to be minimised. The general procedure for dealing with minimisation problems is no different from maximisation problems. A feasible region will still be obtained but instead of moving your isocost line away from the origin, you will be moving it towards the origin.

There must have to be, of course, at least one greater than or equal to constraint otherwise you will arrive at the origin!

Example 2

Ratkins a local DIY store has decided to advertise on television and radio but is unsure about the number of adverts it should place. It wishes to minimise the total cost of the campaign and has limited the total number of 'slots' to no more than 5. However, it wants to have at least one slot on both media. The company has been told that one T.V slot will be seen by 1 million viewers, while a slot on local radio will only be heard by 100,000 listeners. The company wishes to reach an audience of at least 2 million people. If the cost of advertising is £5000 for each radio slot and £20,000 for each T.V slot, how should it advertise?

This problem can be solved by the graphical method of linear programming because there are two variables; the number of radio adverts and the number of T.V adverts.

Activity 18

Formulate the problem given in Example 2.

The formulation for this problem is as follows.

Let R = No. of radio ads and T = No. of T.V ads

Min $5000R + 20000T$

Subject to:

$$0.1R + T \geq 2 \quad \text{(Minimum audience in millions)}$$
$$R + T \leq 5 \quad \text{(Maximum number of 'slots')}$$
$$R \geq 1 \quad \text{(At least one slot on both)}$$
$$T \geq 1$$

Activity 19

Solve this problem using the graphical method. Is the solution sensible?

The procedure for drawing the graph is the same as for the maximising case. That is, it is necessary to find the points at which the constraints cuts the axes. The following table gives these values.

Constraint	R	T
Audience	20	2
Total slots	5	5
Min slots for radio	1	0
Min slots for TV	0	1

The graph for this problem is shown in Figure 7, below. You should confirm that the feasible region is given by the area enclosed by ABC. The optimum point will be at one of these corners and this time it is necessary for you to find the point that gives the minimum value. You should have found that the coordinates and hence cost at each of the corner points are as follows:

	R	T	Cost
A	1	1.9	£43,000
B	1	4	£85,000
C	3.33	1.67	£50,050

Point A gives the minimum cost of £43,000. This solution implies that the company should buy 1 radio advert and 1.9 T.V adverts, hardly a sensible solution. Unfortunately linear programming will give fractional values and if this is not sensible integer linear programming should be used. This technique is not covered in this book but for two variable problems a more realistic solution can often be found by inspecting the graph. In this particular case it is simply a matter of rounding the 1.9 to 2, which increases the cost to £45,000. However, do take care as rounding can often give you an infeasible solution. This can be avoided by checking to see that all constraints are still satisfied. In this example $R = 1$ and $T = 2$ does satisfy all 4 constraints.

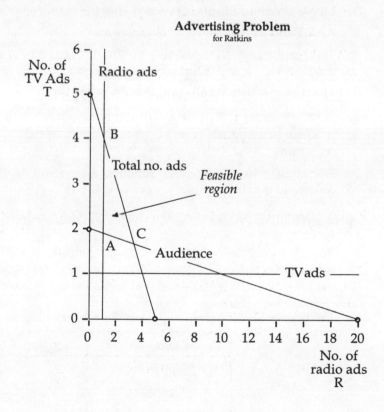

Advertising Problem
for Ratkins

Figure 7

4.10 Summary

This chapter introduced you to a very important technique called linear programming. This technique is typically used when a number of products share the same scarce resources. However, linear programming can be used for a wide variety of problems such as blending problems, capital rationing, transportation problems etc.

Two variable problems can be solved by a graphical method but larger problems require the use of a computer package. Sensitivity analysis can be applied to L.P solutions and this will give you information concerning the marginal value of a resource and the sensitivity of the solution to changes of the objective coefficients.

4.11 Further reading

Oakshott, L, *Quantitative Approaches to Decision Making*, DP Publications, 1993, Unit 18.

Lucey, T, *Quantitative Techniques*, DP Publications, 1992, Chapters 17 and 18.

Anderson, Sweeney and Williams, *An Introduction to Management Science*. West Publishing Company, 1994, Chapter 3.

4.12 Exercises

Progress questions

These question have been designed to help you remember the key points in this chapter. The answers to these questions are given in Appendix 1, page 108.

Give the missing word in each case:

1. Linear programming is concerned with the management of .... resources.

2. An L.P model consists of an objective and a series of linear ....

3. The graphical method of linear programming can be used to solve .... variable problems.

4. The region satisfying all constraints is called the .... region.

5. The optimal solution of an L.P model lies at the corner point of the .... region.

6. A constraint that has reached its limit at the optimal solution is called a .... constraint.

7. The change in the objective function as a result in the unit change of a tight constraint is called the .... price.

Answer TRUE or FALSE

8. You can only solve L.P problems graphically if there are no more than two constraints.

    True ☐ False ☐

9. The line connecting points with equal profit is called an isoprofit line

    True ☐ False ☐

10. The line $X + Y = 10$ is a horizontal line

    True ☐ False ☐

11. A feasible region must be bounded on all sides by constraints.

    True ☐ False ☐

Review questions

These questions have been designed to help you check your comprehension of the key points in this chapter. You may wish to look further than this chapter in order to answer them fully. You will find the reading list useful in this respect. You can check the essential elements of your answers by referring to the appropriate section.

12. Why is not possible to use the graphical technique to solve an L.P problem with more than two variables? (Section 4.2)

13. How important is it to draw a graph for two variable problems? (Section 4.4)

14. Describe the essential differences between a maximisation problem and a minimisation problem. (Sections 4.3 and 4.9)

15. What is the purpose of sensitivity analysis in linear programming? (Section 4.8)

Multiple choice questions

The answers to these will be given in the Lecturers' Supplement.

16. The line $Y = 7$ has a gradient of:
    A 1
    B 7
    C 0

17. The line $Y + 3X = 9$ passes through the point:
    A (0,9)
    B (9,0)
    C (0,3)

18. To solve an L.P model graphical it is best if the scales on each axes are:
    A The same
    B Different
    C Both start at zero

19. A tight constraint will have a shadow price of:
    A Zero
    B More than zero
    C The value of the right hand side of the constraint

Practice questions

Answers to these questions will be given in the Lecturers' Supplement.

20. A particular linear programming problem is formulated as follows:

    Min $Z = 2500x + 3500y$

    Subject to:

    $$5x + 6y \geq 250$$
    $$4x + 3y \geq 150$$
    $$x + 2y \geq 70$$
    $$x, y \geq 0$$

Draw these constraints on graph paper and determine the optimum solution.

21. Gnomes United currently make two types of garden gnomes called Digger and Fisher. You have been asked to decide on the number of each gnome to make during an 8 week period in order to maximise contribution to fixed costs and profits.

    Using the information below, formulate a linear programming model.

    Resource requirements:

	Digger	Fisher
Material (kg)	0.25	0.33
Unskilled labour (mins)	1.75	3.00
Skilled labour (mins)	3.00	4.00

    Resource availabilities:

    Material in stock: 20,000kg

    Labour: 9 unskilled workers and 13 skilled workers

	Digger	Fisher
Variable cost of manufacture	£1.70	£2.20
Selling Price	£3.00	£4,00

    You can assume a 100% conversion factor for materials and labour works at 100% efficiency. All employees work a 40 hour week and can work on either product.

22. A company has been set up in Bristol to manufacture rowing dinghies. Currently they have plans to produce a basic and a deluxe version. The two dinghies are similar and both take 1.5 man-days to manufacture. However, the deluxe version is much stronger and the profit is higher as can be seen in the table below:

	Basic	Deluxe
Resin	10 kgms	16 kgms
Glass Fibre Mat	30 m	50 m
Profit	£50	£80

    Due to safety regulations the company is only allowed to store a limited amount of the raw material, which is 200 kgms of resin and 900 m of mat. The required raw material is delivered on a daily basis.

    The basic dinghy is likely to be a good seller but it is assumed that the deluxe dinghy will be limited to a maximum of nine per day. All boats produced by the end of the day are delivered to a distribution depot as there are no storage facilities available at the Plant.

    a) If the current labour force is 27, use the graphical method of linear programming to demonstrate that there are multiple solutions to the problem. Hence suggest a sensible mix of dinghies to produce on a daily basis and show that this results in a profit of £1,000 per day.

b) i) What is the Shadow Price of the resin resource?

   ii) As a result of improved storage facilities more resin can be held at the plant. What is the maximum amount of resin that would be worth storing and how would this affect the profit calculated in (a)?

23. Revor plc has one production line for the manufacture of the ELEN PLUS and ELEN SUPER ignition systems. Both models use similar components in their manufacture but the SUPER model usually requires more of them and takes longer to produce. Relevant detail is shown below.

	ELEN PLUS	ELEN SUPER
No. of component A	4	8
No. of component B	2	3
No. of component C	0	10
Manufacturing time(hours)	5	7

There are supply problems for components A and B and daily usage is limited to 400 and 250 respectively. For component C, the company has entered into a contract with its supplier to take at least 150 per day.

It is also found that at least twice as many ELEN PLUS models are sold as ELEN SUPER, so production should reflect this fact.

The contribution to profits for the PLUS and SUPER models are £60 and £85 respectively.

You can assume that there are 60 employees engaged in the production of these ignition systems and each employee works an 8 hour day.

a) Formulate this as a linear programming problem, assuming that it is required to maximise profits.

b) Use the graphical technique of linear programming to determine the optimal numbers of ELEN PLUS and ELEN SUPER models to produce each day. What is the daily profit associated with this production?

c) Identify the scarce resources (binding constraints) for this problem. For each determine the shadow price. It is possible to purchase additional quantities of component A from an alternative supplier at a premium of £10 per component. Would it be worthwhile?

d) The unit costs associated with the production of these systems is known to vary. However the selling price is only changed annually. How much can the profit on the ELEN PLUS model be allowed to vary before the optimal solution found in (b) changes?

Assignment

Answers to this assignment are included in the Lecturers' supplement.

The Food department at Riglen plc has brought out a new breakfast cereal called Hi-Fibre, which uses a concentrated form of fibre developed by Riglen's research laboratory. This product has been test marketed in a few selected areas and the consumer reaction has been favourable. However several people questioned said that they would prefer a higher fibre content, so Dave Smith, the Product manager has decided to meet this demand with an additional product called Hi-Fibre Plus. This product will have double the fibre content of Hi-Fibre and will require additional cooking time. The selling price of Hi-Fibre Plus will be greater than for Hi-Fibre and the contribution to profits also will be higher. For Hi-Fibre, the contribution will be 12p per 500g packet, and for Hi-Fibre Plus it will be 15p per 500g packet.

During the period of test marketing, 500 packets of the product were produced each day. However from a commercial point of view at least 2500 packets of each product must be produced daily and it is expected that demand will soon exceed this figure. Dave's problem is that he is unsure of the quantities of each product to produce. Even if he assumes that he can sell all that he makes, the resources at his disposal are limited. The storage area can take a maximum of 12,000 packets so total daily production of the cereal cannot exceed this figure. He has one oven and one packaging plant that operates for twelve hours a day and the supply of concentrated fibre is, for the moment, restricted to 120kg per day. There is no practical limit to the other ingredients.

Dave Smith has asked you to use the technique of linear programming to solve his production problem and he has given you the following additional information:

	Hi-Fibre	Hi-Fibre Plus
Cooking/packaging	3 seconds	5 seconds
Fibre content	5g	10g

All figures are based on 500g of cereal.

a) Formulate this problem in L.P terms with the objective of maximising contribution to profits.

b) Use the graphical technique of linear programming to solve this problem.

c) How much of each resource (that is fibre, storage space and the working day) is left after the optimal quantities of cereal are produced? Which resources are 'scarce'? (that is, all used up).

d) Is it worthwhile increasing any of the scarce resources? and by how much? The additional cost of increasing fibre production is £20 per kg, storage space would work out at 20p per packet and extending the working day would incur costs of £30 per hour.

e) Would the optimal solution change if the profit contribution of either product changed?

f) The Sales department believes that the demand for Hi-fibre Plus will be greater than for Hi-Fibre. If this is correct production of Hi-Fibre Plus needs to be higher than Hi-Fibre. What increase in profit contribution of Hi-Fibre Plus will be necessary if the total profit is to remain the same?

5 Critical path analysis

5.1 Introduction

Whenever a large or complex project is undertaken a great deal of planning is necessary. Building a house is a good example as there are many tasks or activities that have to be completed, some of which can proceed at the same time while others have to wait until preceding tasks are completed. Without careful planning, you might find that materials for a particular activity are not delivered on time or an electrician is not available when he is required. Delays in the project would result and you would find that the cost is far higher than it should be. This chapter introduces a number of techniques that are used in the planning and control of large projects.

On completing this chapter you should be able to:

❑ Construct an 'activity-on-node' network to represent a project.

❑ Calculate the earliest and latest start and finish times for each activity.

❑ Calculate the float for each activity and identify the critical path.

❑ Use a Gantt chart and resource histogram to smooth the use of resources required by a project.

❑ Apply the technique of cost scheduling.

5.2 The activity-on-node method

This technique allows the time of the project and the slack (or float) of individual activities to be determined. If an activity has zero float you would say that it was critical because any delay in that activity would delay the entire project.

Before critical path analysis (or CPA) is used it is first necessary to make a list of all the activities, their durations and which activities must immediately precede them.

Example 1

You have just obtained planning permission to build a garage and you are now in the process of planning the project. With a little help from a friendly builder you have made a list of activities that need to be completed, the durations of these activities and the order which they can be tackled. This list is shown below.

Activity	Description	Immediate preceding activities	Duration (Days)
A	Obtain bricklayer	–	10
B	Dig the foundations	–	8
C	Lay the base	B	1
D	Build the walls	A and C	8
E	Build the roof	D	3
F	Tile the roof	E	2
G	Make window frames	–	3
H	Fit the window frames	D and G	1
I	Fit glass to frames	H	1
J	Fit the door	E	1
K	Paint the door and window frames	I and J	2
L	Point the brickwork	D	2

Once this list has been completed, you should represent the project by the means of a diagram. The diagram used in this book uses the activity-on-node method. The basic diagram for this method is shown below. The nodes represent the activity and the lines the dependencies between activities.

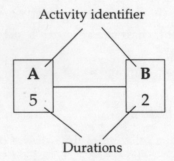

Activity identifier

Durations

Figure 1 Activity-on-node

Activity 1

Draw the network for the garage problem using the activity-on-node method.

The basic diagram for the garage problem is shown below. You will see that the name of each activity is displayed in the box together with the duration. You will also see that there are start and end nodes. This is to ensure that every activity has at least one line entering and one line leaving its node.

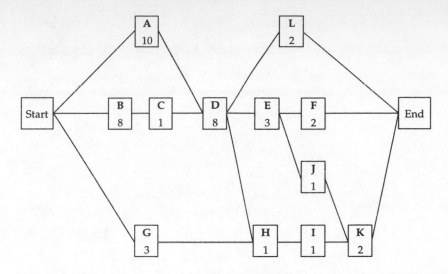

Figure 2 The garage problem

For this method you need to display 4 additional pieces of information on each node. They are the earliest start time of the activity (EST), the latest start time (LST), the earliest finish time (EFT), and the latest finish time (LFT). This information should be displayed as follows.

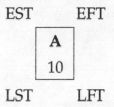

Figure 3

In order to calculate the EST and EFT a forward pass is made through the network. If the start is at time zero then the EST of activities A, B and G is zero and their EFT is 10, 8 and 3 respectively. The EST of activity C must be 8 since it can start as soon as B is completed. However what about activity D? This activity cannot start until both A and C are completed and as A is completed later than C then activity A determines the EST of D, which must be 10. This is the general rule when calculating the EST – if there are two or more choices the EST is the larger of the EFT's of the preceding activities. From this you will see that the EST of K must be 22 and not 20.

Activity 2

Continue the forward pass through the network and add this information to your network. How long will it take you to complete the project?

You can now check your answers with the diagram below. From this diagram you will see that the project will take 24 days in total.

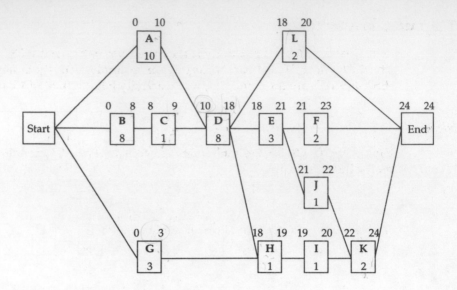

Figure 4

To enable the LFT and LST to be calculated a backward pass is made through the network, starting at the END node. The LFT of activity F, K and L must be 24 since the project is only complete when all these activities have been completed. The LST of F, K and L must all be 22 days since the duration of all three activities is 2 days. To calculate the LFT of all other activities involves a process similar to that for the forward pass, with one difference, which is, that when there is a choice the smallest value is chosen.

Activity 3

Continue the backward pass through the network.

Figure 5 shows the completed network.

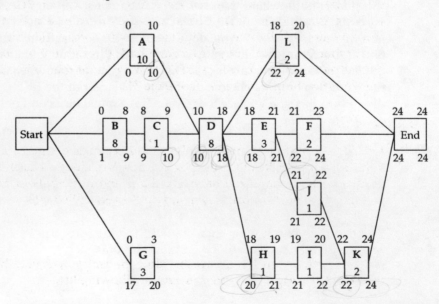

Figure 5 The completed network

5.3 The float of an activity

The float or slack of an activity is the difference between the EST and LST (or between the EFT and LFT) for each activity. For example, activity D has zero float since the EST and LST are the same (10), while activity F has a float of 1 day (22 – 21).

Activity 4

Obtain the floats for the remainder of the activities. Which activities are 'critical', that is have no float?

You should have obtained the following results:

Activity	EST	LST	Float
A	0	0	0
B	0	1	1
C	8	9	1
D	10	10	0
E	18	18	0
F	21	22	1
G	0	17	17
H	18	20	2
I	19	21	2
J	21	21	0
K	22	22	0
L	18	22	4

From this you can see that activities A, D, E, J and K have zero float and are therefore critical . Any delay in the start or finish times of these activities would delay the entire project by the same amount. The other activities could be delayed by up to their float without affecting the overall project time. For example activity B (dig foundations) could be delayed by one day but this activity would then become critical. You will notice that the critical activities form a path through the network – this is called the critical path. However, it is possible to have more than one critical path as you will see when crashing is looked at (see page 74).

5.4 Resource scheduling

Activities of a project often involve resources of one kind or another. In the garage building example, labour is the obvious resource since each activity requires people to do the work. Perhaps you have asked a friend or neighbour to help and the two of you intend to help the bricklayer and do the less skilled jobs.

Example 2

For each activity in the garage building project you decide how many people are required to do these jobs and you get the following list.

Activity	No. of people required
A	0
B	2
C	2
D	1
E	1
F	2
G	1
H	1
I	1
J	2
K	1
L	1

Since some activities, such as digging the foundations and making the window frames can take place at the same time, the number of people required at a particular time may be greater than the availability. However it may be possible to delay non-critical activities such as making the window frames sufficiently to avoid this problem. The critical path network cannot easily solve this problem because this network is designed to show the order in which activities take place rather than when they take place. A better chart to use is the Gantt chart. A Gantt chart is like a bar chart that has been turned on its side. The horizontal axis is time and each activity is represented by a bar, the start of the bar is initially the EST and the end of the bar is the EFT. The float of an activity is represented by a dotted line.

Activity 5

Draw the Gantt chart for the garage project.

This chart is shown in Figure 6, below.

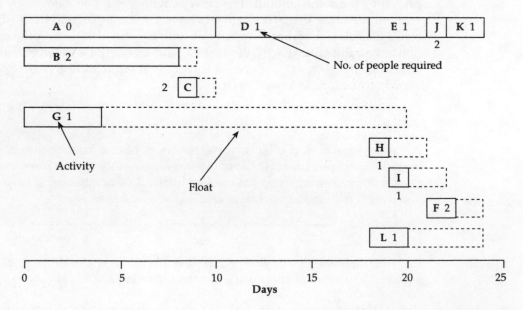

Figure 6 The Gantt chart

You will see that the bars representing the critical activities have all been placed on one line – this is because each activity follows one another on the critical path. The non-critical activities should however be placed on separate lines so that their floats can be clearly shown. The number of people required has been added to each bar. From this you can see that 3 people are required during the first 3 days (0 + 2 + 1).

Activity 6

Repeat this procedure for the entire project. When are more than 2 people required?

The figures are:

Day	Number of people required
1–3	3
4–8	2
9–10	0
11–18	1
19–20	3
21	1
22	4
23	3
24	1

Where you can see that more that 2 people are required on several occasions (4 people are required on day 22). You might find this easier to see on the *resource histogram* in Figure 7, below.

Resource histogram

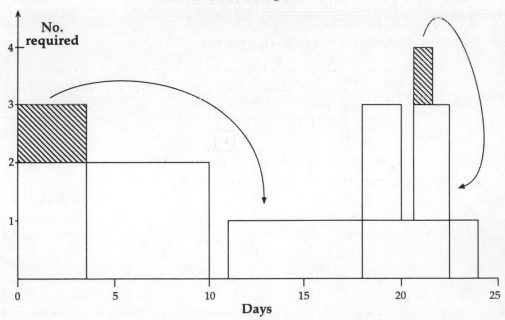

Figure 7 The resource histogram

From this histogram you will see clearly the peaks and troughs in the resource requirements. If a peak could be moved into a trough the net result would be a smoother histogram which is the point of the exercise. A perfectly smooth histogram would mean that the resource is being fully utilised and no further savings would be possible. In the case of the garage it would be possible to delay the start of activity G (make window frames) until day 9 since G has a float of 17 days. This would mean that from the start of the project until day 12 two people would be required all the time. (The smoothing is shown using shading on the histogram). The peaks at the end of the project is not so easy to solve. If the start of activity F (tile the roof) was delayed by its float of one day, the peak of four people during day 22 could be reduced by one. So three people are required for much of the latter part of the project. The alternative to increasing the number of people is to extend the project. For example if the critical activities J (fitting the door) and K (painting) were delayed for three days the project would be delayed by this amount of time but you would then find that the project could be completed with 2 people for the entire 27 days.

5.5 Cost scheduling

A very important resource in network analysis is money. This resource is usually so important that a separate technique has been devised to solve problems posed by financial considerations. This technique is called crashing.

It is usually desirable to reduce the time a project takes because there are often financial advantages in doing so. For example, the Department of Transport pays a bonus to contractors who complete a road building or repair project early. (And a penalty is charged if the project time is over-run). It is often possible to speed up the completion of an activity at an extra cost. This cost may be because a machine is hired or because more people are employed. The reduced duration is called the crashed duration and the increased cost is called the crashed cost.

Example 3

It is possible to reduce the time for completing activities B, D, E, F, G, K and L of the garage building project by employing additional labour. If this is done costs will increase for these activities. The table below gives you the durations and costs for all activities.

Activity duration (days)	Normal duration (days)	Crash cost	Normal cost	Crash
A	10	10	£5	£5
B	8	2	£100	£700
C	1	1	£200	£200
D	8	5	£800	£1700
E	3	2	£500	£900
F	2	1	£200	£400
G	3	1	£150	£550
H	1	1	£50	£50
I	1	1	£20	£20
J	1	1	£20	£20
K	2	1	£30	£130
L	2	1	£100	£200

Activity 7

What is the normal total cost of the project?

The total cost is simply the sum of all the activities, since all must be completed. This is £2170. If some of the activities are crashed this cost will increase. The question is which activities should be crashed in order to reduce the project time to a minimum but without incurring unnecessary costs

Activity 8

Would it be worth crashing all the activities identified above?

The answer to this question is no because not all the activities are on the critical path. Even if they were, some of the activities are more economic to crash than others. For instance activity D costs £300 per day to crash (an extra cost of £900 and a time reduction of 3 days) while activity E costs £400 per day. The objective of crashing should be to find the minimum project duration at the minimum extra cost. In order to satisfy this objective it is first necessary to find the cost per day of all activities. This is necessary as the crashing can make non-critical activities become critical.

Activity 9

Calculate the cost per day for the relevant activities specified in Example 3.

This calculation is summarised in the table below.

Activity (days)	Time reduction	Extra cost	Cost/day
B	6	£600	£100
D	3	£900	£300
E	1	£400	£400
F	1	£200	£200
G	2	£400	£200
K	1	£100	£100
L	1	£100	£100

The next step is to write down all the paths through the network together with their durations. (Path GHIK can be ignored because it has a relatively short duration).

Activity 10

Make a list of all major paths through the network.

You should have found 8 major paths, which are given as follows:

Path	Duration
ADEJK	24
BCDEJK	23
ADEF	23
ADHIK	22
BCDEF	22
BCDHIK	21
ADL	20
BCDL	19

Path ADEJK must be reduced first because it is the longest path through the network and therefore the critical path. Activities D, E and K can be crashed but of the three K is the cheapest. If K is crashed by one day then not only will the duration of path ADEJK be reduced by one but so will paths BCDEJK, ADHIK and BCDHIK. The project duration has now been reduced by one day at a cost of £100 but path ADEF is now critical, in addition to ADEJK. These two paths must now be crashed together. Both D and E are common to these two paths and since D is the cheapest, this will be crashed by three days at a cost of £900. Finally E is crashed by one day to reduce the project duration to 19 days at an extra cost of £1400. No further crashing is worthwhile because it is not possible to crash both critical paths (only F has any crashing capability left). You might find it easier to write the necessary steps in a table similar to the one below.

Path	Duration	Step 1	Step 2	Step3
ADEJK	24	23	20	19
BCDEJK	23	22	19	18
ADEF	23	23	20	19
ADHIK	22	21	18	18
BCDEF	22	22	19	18
BCDHIK	21	20	17	17
ADL	20	20	17	17
BCDL	19	19	16	16
Activities crashed		K–1	D–3	E–1
Extra cost		£100	£900	£400
Cumulative extra cost		£100	£1000	£1400

Is it worthwhile reducing the project time by 5 days at an extra cost of £1400? It may be that you are paying someone by the day to help you and any reduction in time would save you this 'overhead' charge. For example, suppose you were paying this person £150 per day. It would be worthwhile crashing K because for an expenditure of £100 you would save £150; a net gain of £50. However it wouldn't be worthwhile crashing D because for each day saved it has cost you £150 (£300 – £150).

5.6 Summary

This chapter introduced you to some very useful techniques for planning and monitoring a project that involves many inter-dependent activities. The activity-on-node method was used to draw the network diagram. From this network it was possible to obtain the total time that the project will take and the floats of each activity. Where an activity has zero float it is called critical and any delay in this activity will delay the entire project. The activity-on-node diagram shows you how the activities are related but it doesn't very easily show you when they occur. The Gantt chart is better for this purpose and this chart can be used to smooth the resources over time. Finally, the technique of crashing was introduced. This technique allows you to speed up a project at minimum extra cost.

5.7 Further reading

Anderson, Sweeney and Williams, *An Introduction to Management Science*, West Publishing Company, 1994, Chapter 10.

Oakshott, L, *Quantitative Approaches to Decision Making*, DP Publications, 1993, Unit 15.

Wisniewski, M, *Quantitative Methods for Decision Making*, Pitman Publishing, 1994, Chapter 13.

5.8 Exercises

Progress questions

These question have been designed to help you remember the key points in this chapter. The answers to these questions are given in Appendix 1, page 108.

Give the missing word in each case:

1. EST stands for Earliest .... time.

2. A .... pass through the network is used to obtain the EST and EFT for each activity.

3. A .... pass through the network is used to obtain the LST and LFT for each activity.

4. A critical activity has .... float.

Answer TRUE or FALSE

5. It is not possible to have more than one critical path in a network.

    True ☐   False ☐

6. All nodes must have at least one line entering and one line leaving.

    True ☐   False ☐

7. Float is the difference between the EST and EFT.

    True ☐   False ☐

8. To reduce the time for a project you must reduce the durations of the critical path

    True ☐   False ☐

Review questions

These questions have been designed to help you check your comprehension of the key points in this chapter. You may wish to look further than this chapter in order to answer them fully. You will find the reading list useful in this respect. You can check the essential elements of your answers by referring to the appropriate section.

9. What are the essential features of the activity-on-node method for representing a project? (Section 5.2)

10. Why is it important to know the critical activities of a project? (Section 5.3)

11. Describe the essential differences between a CPA chart and a Gantt chart. (Sections 5.2 and 5.4)

Multiple choice questions

The answers to these will be given in the Lecturers' Supplement.

12. A Gantt chart is used to:
    A. Show how activities are related
    B. Show when activities take place
    C. Enable the critical path to be evaluated
    D. Show resources used over time

13. A resource histogram is used to:
    A. Show how activities are related
    B. Show when activities take place
    C. Enable the critical path to be evaluated
    D. Show resources used over time

14. Crashing is the term used when:
    A. The project time has to be reduced at minimum extra cost.
    B. Insufficient resources are available for the project to be completed on time.
    C. The cost of a project has to be reduced.

15. If the EST and LST of an activity are 12 and 14 respectively, the float for this activity is:
    A. zero
    B. 2
    C. 26

Practice questions

Answers to these questions will be given in the Lecturers' Supplement.

16. Please refer to the diagram below for this question
    a) How long will the project take?
    b) How much float has activity D?
    c) How much float has activity F?
    d) If activity B takes 3 weeks longer than expected, will the project be delayed?
    e) If activity B requires 3 people continuously, D requires 2 people and C requires 1 person, how many people are required during week 6?

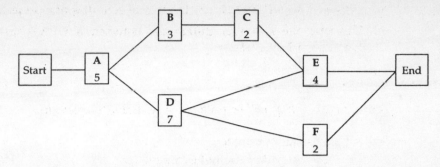

17. Yachtsteer manufacture a self-steering device for pleasure yachts and as a result of increased competition from foreign manufacturers, it has decided to design and manufacture a new model in time for the next Boat show. As a first step in planning the project, the following major tasks and durations have been identified:

	Task	Time (Weeks)	Preceding Tasks
A	Design new product	8	–
B	Design electronics	4	–
C	Organise production facilities	4	A
D	Obtain production materials	2	A
E	Manufacture trial gear	3	C,D
F	Obtain electronic circuit boards	2	B
G	Decide on yacht for trials	1	–
H	Assemble trial gear and electronics	2	E,F
I	Test product in workshops	3	H,G
J	Test product at sea	4	I
K	Assess product's performance	3	J
L	Plan national launch	4	K

Draw a network to represent the logical sequence of tasks and determine how long it will be before the new product can be launched.

18. Shipways boatyard undertakes spring refits on cabin cruisers and yachts and in the past the company has received complaints from customers regarding the time taken to complete the job. As a consequence the M.D, Alan Waters has decided to carry out a critical path analysis on the cabin cruiser refit. Table below gives, for each activity, the duration, immediate preceding activities and the number of yard assistants required.

Activity	Description	Duration (Days)	Immediate preceding activities	Yard assistants required
A	Bring craft up slipway	1	–	2
B	Check and overhaul seacocks etc	3	A	1
C	Scrape and prepare hull for painting	7	A	2
D	Paint hull	4	C	1
E	Remove engine	2	A	3
F	Overhaul engine	16	E	1
G	Clean and paint engine bilges	3	E	1
H	Refit engine	3	F and G	3
I	Apply antifoul paint to hull	2	D and H	2
J	Refloat	1	B and I	2

Note. The reason that I follows from both D and H is that a boat must be refloated no more than 48 hours after the antifouling paint has been applied. Antifouling should not therefore be started until the boat is ready for the water.

a) Draw the network and determine how long the refit will take. What are the critical activities and how much float do the non-critical activities have?

b) i) Draw a Gantt chart and resource histogram for the refit. What is the maximum number of yard workers required and when is this required?

ii) Unfortunately there are only 4 yard workers available during the period of the refit. Using your Gantt chart and/or histogram reschedule the activities so that no more than 4 yard workers will be required.

19. Revor plc are urgently planning the production of their new light weight car battery, the 'Epsilon'. They would like to exhibit their battery at a trade fair, which is to take place in 48 weeks time. Various activities had to take place before production could start and these are shown below:

	Task	Time (Weeks)	Preceding Tasks
A	Design new product	8	–
B	Design electronics	4	–
A	Clear designated area for the installation of equipment	–	20
B	Commission consulting engineers to design equipment	–	2
C	Receive consultant's report	B	10
D	Place equipment out to tender	C	1
E	Obtain equipment	D	6
F	Install equipment	A,E	30
G	Recruit additional staff	C	6
H	Train new staff	G	4
I	Order and obtain materials	–	16
J	Pilot production run	F,H,I	3
K	Advertise new product	–	2

a) Draw the network and show that it is not possible to start production within 48 weeks. What are the critical activities and how much total float do the non-critical activities have?

b) It is possible to 'crash' (i.e. reduce the duration of) certain activities at increased cost. These activities are as follows:

Activity	Crashed Duration (Weeks)	Normal Cost (£000's)	Crashed Cost (£000's)
A	18	4	10
E	5	1	3
F	28	15	27
I	8	0.5	8.5
J	2	16	26

i) Ron Smith the Production Manager suggests that only activity I need be crashed because this is the cheapest option and allows the greatest reduction in time to be made. Explain why this would not help the situation.

ii) It has been estimated that for every week over 48 weeks that this project takes, a loss of £8000 is made as a result of lost profits. Decide on the strategy that will minimise the sum of crashed costs and loss of profits.

Assignment

Answers to this assignment are included in the Lecturer's supplement.

There have been recurring problems with the food canning process at Riglen plc and a decision has been taken at Board level to replace the machinery with more modern computer controlled equipment. Holder and Holder Consulting Engineers have been commissioned to advise on the system to purchase and their report is expected in 5 weeks time. Although the fine details of the recommended system will not be known until this report has been received, the essential characteristics of all the alternatives are the same. Planning for the installation can therefore start immediately and this is important because during the installation all food canning has to be contracted out and this will be expensive.

In order to ensure that the project is completed as quickly as possible and at minimum cost you have been asked to use the relevant network analysis techniques on the data given below. You should also note that fitters are to be employed on a fixed term contract and it is important that only the minimum number necessary are recruited.

Activity	Description	Duration (weeks)	Immediate Predecessors	Fitters required	Cost (£000's)
A	Obtain consulting engineer's report	5	–	0	5
B	Remove existing machinery	4	–	8	3
C	Purchase new machinery	5	A	0	50
D	Purchase electrics	7	A	0	15
E	Purchase computers	6	A	0	25
F	Install machinery	4	B and C	5	5
G	Install computers	3	E	3	5
H	Connect electrics	3	F and D	2	4
I	Recruit and train staff	6	–	0	3
J	Pilot production run	1	G and H	6	6
K	Prepare for full production	4	I and J	5	2

a) Draw the network and calculate the start and finish times for each activity. How long will the project take and what are the critical activities?

b) Draw a Gantt chart for this project. What is the maximum number of fitters required and during what weeks does this occur. What is the minimum number of fitters required that will still allow the project to be completed in the time found in (i) above?

c) An attempt is to be made to reduce the total project time since for every weeks reduction a saving of £10,000 can be achieved through not having to contract out the weeks canning. This will be possible because some activities such as B can be completed in less time than scheduled. Of course this reduction in time will be at an increased cost.

The activities that can be reduced (crashed) in time are given below.

Activity	Normal time (weeks)	Crashed time (weeks)	Normal cost (£000's)	Crashed cost (£000's)
B	4	2	10	16
D	7	6	15	21
F	6	3	5	20
G	3	2	5	12
K	4	3	2	10

i) What is the total normal cost of the project including the £10,000 per week canning charge?

ii) Using the figures above, calculate for each activity the cost of reducing the time by one week.

iii) Starting with the critical path, make a list of all paths through the network. Alongside each path write down the duration in weeks of the path.

iv) Try and reduce the critical path to the same duration as the next largest in the cheapest way possible. Now reduce both paths until the duration is equal to the next highest path and so on. Repeat this until no more reduction is possible. What is the new total cost of the project?

v) What is the project duration that will minimise the total cost of the project?

6 *Inventory control*

6.1 *Introduction*

Holding stock is a very expensive business particularly where the goods are of high value. However even for small value items the cost can be high if the quantities involved are large enough. This chapter looks at some methods for determining the cheapest stock control policies. You will find it useful to have some knowledge of the normal distribution for section 6.5 of this chapter.

On completing this chapter you should be able to:

❐ Calculate the costs associated with holding stocks.

❐ Calculate the order quantity that minimises these costs.

❐ Decide whether buying in bulk to obtain a price discount is worthwhile.

❐ Calculate a buffer stock to avoid stock-outs.

❐ Appreciate the limitations of the EOQ model.

6.2 *Costs of holding stock*

There are many costs associated with holding (or not holding) stock. Some of these are:

❐ warehouse costs

❐ money tied up in stock (interest charges)

❐ damage while in storage

❐ deterioration while in storage

❐ obsolescence

❐ ordering costs

❐ delivery costs

❐ cost of any 'stock-outs'

Warehouse costs include things like rental charges, heating and wages. Money that is tied up in stock could be earning money (or reduce overdraft charges). A certain proportion of goods will be damaged while in the warehouse or may be stolen and certain products deteriorate (for example food) while other items may become obsolete if stored too long (last years computer will be worth less than the latest version). In addition to the costs directly associated with the holding of stock there is also the cost of ordering and delivery. Most large companies will have a buying department and this means that there must be a cost associated with ordering. Even if only telephone and postage were costed, each order would still cost a finite amount. Finally there is a cost of a 'stock-out'. If the computer game store 'Game World' sells computer games and reckons to make, say £30 on a sale of a particular game, then for each sale that cannot be fulfilled the company will lose this profit. Not only will they lose this sale but they may lose future sales because potential customers may decide to go to stores that always have adequate stock.

If the case for and against holding stock can be resolved on cost alone then it is a matter of minimising the total cost associated with an inventory policy. There are many inventory control models that do this, some are quite simple deterministic models while others can accommodate uncertainty or handle many different goods at the same time. For particularly complex inventory control systems, simulation may be used to arrive at the best policy. (See Chapter 7, page 97).

All models will tell you how much to order and when to order. The simplest model is the Economic Order Quantity model, which will now be described.

6.3 The Economic Order Quantity (EOQ) Model

The assumptions that have to be made before this model can be used are as follows:

- ❏ Demand is known and constant.
- ❏ Lead time is constant.
- ❏ Only one item is involved.
- ❏ Stock is monitored on a continuous basis and an order is made when the stock level reaches a re-order point.
- ❏ When an order arrives, the stock level is replenished instantaneously.
- ❏ Stock-outs do not occur

Figure 1, below may help you picture the general problem. An order quantity Q arrives and is used up at a constant rate, until the stock level reaches zero, at which point a new order arrives.

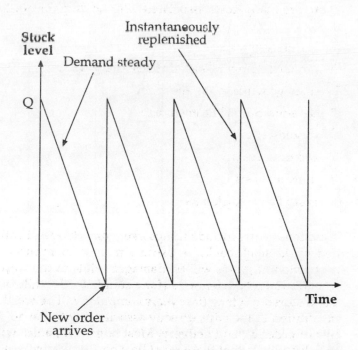

Figure 1

For small values of Q more frequent ordering will be necessary and hence order costs will be high, while large values of Q will increase the quantity in store and therefore increase the storage costs. The problem is to determine the value of Q that minimises the sum of the order and storage costs.

If the cost of placing an order is represented by the letter c, then the total order cost is simply the number of orders made multiplied by c. If D is the demand over a specified time period then the number of orders made must be:

$$\frac{D}{Q}$$

and the order cost is:

$$c \times \frac{D}{Q}$$

To calculate the storage cost it is assumed that the cost of holding one unit in stock for a specified time period is known. This cost is represented by h. As the amount in stock varies the average stock level is required and you will see from Figure 2 that this must be

$$\frac{Q}{2}$$

Hence the storage cost is:

$$h \times \frac{Q}{2}$$

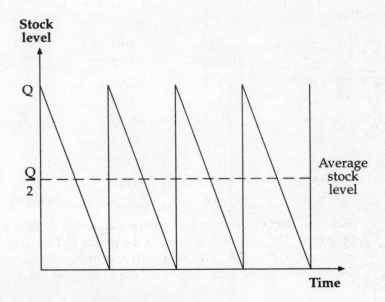

Figure 2

Example

Imagine that you work for 'Game World' and you have been asked to decide on the best inventory control policy for the computer game 'Aliens'. You are told that the demand is fairly constant at 5000 units p.a and it costs £14.40 to place an order. You are also told that the storage cost of holding one unit of the game per annum is £10.

In order to investigate how inventory costs vary with order size you decide to work out the order and storage costs for different order quantities.

For an order size of 20:

Order cost $\qquad = C \times \dfrac{D}{Q}$

$\qquad\qquad\qquad = 14.4 \times \dfrac{5000}{20}$

Total cost $\qquad = £3600$ p.a

Storage cost $\qquad = h \times \dfrac{Q}{2}$

$\qquad\qquad\qquad = 10 \times \dfrac{20}{2}$

$\qquad\qquad\qquad = £100$ p.a

Total cost $\qquad = £3700$ p.a

Activity 1

Repeat this calculation for order quantities from 40 to 200 units.

The results of the calculations are shown in the table below:

Q	Order cost (£)	Storage cost (£)	Total cost (£)
20	3600.0	100.0	3700.0
40	1800.0	200.0	2000.0
60	1200.0	300.0	1500.0
80	900.0	400.0	1300.0
100	720.0	500.0	1220.0
120	600.0	600.0	1200.0
140	514.3	700.0	1214.3
160	450.0	800.0	1250.0
180	400.0	900.0	1300.0
200	360.0	1000.0	1360.0

From this table it appears that an order quantity of 120 gives the lowest total costs at £1200 p.a. This can best be seen in the graph in Figure 3, below. You will also probably notice that the total cost curve is fairly flat around the minimum so that departing from the order size of 120 does not incur much additional cost.

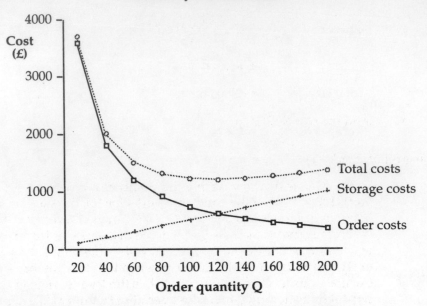

Figure 3

Is it necessary to repeat this analysis each time? Fortunately not, as there is an algebraic formula that can be used to work out the optimum order quantity. The mathematics behind the formula is beyond the scope of this book but you will see from the graph that at minimum cost the order cost and storage cost lines intersect. This means that the two costs are equal at the optimum. This is generally true so:

$$C \times \frac{D}{Q} = h \times \frac{Q}{2}$$

Multiplying both sides by 2Q and rearranging gives you:

$$Q^2 = 2 \times c \times \frac{D}{h}$$

That is: $Q = \sqrt{\dfrac{2cD}{h}}$

This formula is known as the economic order quantity or EOQ and in words it means:

$$\sqrt{\frac{2 \times \text{order cost per order} \times \text{demand}}{\text{holding cost per unit}}}$$

All you have to do to use this formula is simply substitute the values for *c*, *D*, and *h*.

Activity 2

Use the EOQ formula to calculate the value of Q that minimises the sum of the ordering and holding costs. What is this cost?

Your calculations should have been as follows:

That is: $$Q = \sqrt{\frac{2 \times 14.40 \times 5000}{10}}$$

$$= \sqrt{14400}$$

$$= 120$$

And the cost is £1200 p.a.

6.3.1 Time between orders and the re-order level

In the 'Game World' example the number of orders per year at the EOQ of 120 is 5000/120 = 41.67. If the company works for 300 days a year this means that the time between orders should be 300/41.67 = 7.2 days on average.

From Figure 1, page 85, you will see that a new order arrives just as the stock level reaches zero. For this to happen an order must have been placed sometime previously. In practise an order is placed when the stock reaches a predetermined level. To calculate this level all that is required is the lead (or delivery) time. If the lead time is say 4 days then during this time a certain amount of stock will have been sold. With a demand of 5000 a year, the daily sales will be 5000/300 = 16.7 on average. In 4 days, 66.8 or about 67 games will be sold and therefore an order will need to be placed when the stock is down to this level. This re-order level is shown in Figure 4, below.

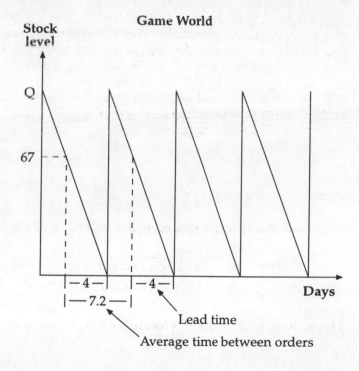

Figure 4

89

Calculate the re-order level for 'Aliens' if the lead time increased to 5 days.

In this case the re-order level should be 5 × 16.7 = 83.5, or about 84 games.

6.4 Discounts

The EOQ is not always the cheapest quantity to purchase. It is often found that discounts are given by the manufacturer or supplier if a certain minimum quantity of goods are bought. In these cases it is necessary to add the cost of the goods to the order and storage costs in order to arrive at the cheapest policy.

Activity 4

You can purchase the computer game 'Aliens' for £50 each but if you order in quantities of 500 or more a 5% discount is given. Should you take advantage of this discount?

To answer this question you need to add the product cost to the cost of ordering and storage. At the EOQ (120), the product cost is:

5000 × £50 = £250,000

and the storage and order cost is £1200 (see page 89)

The total cost is therefore: 250,000 + 1200 = £251,200

If 500 is purchased at a time, the order and storage will change and the unit cost will fall to £50 − £2.50 = £47.50, so

Order cost	$£14.40 \times \dfrac{5000}{500}$	=	£144
Storage cost	$£10 \times \dfrac{500}{2}$	=	£2,500
Product cost	5000 × £47.50	=	£237,500
Total cost		=	£240,144

By ordering in quantities of 500 a saving of £11,056 p.a (£251,200 − £240,144) can be realised.

6.5 Uncertainty in demand

The EOQ model assumes that the demand for the product is known and constant. This assumption is unlikely to be valid in practise, and the demand is likely to fluctuate from day to day. Rather than scrap this model completely it is possible, with further assumptions, to compensate for this variability.

Assuming that you are operating a re-order level system (that is, the stock level is continuously monitored) any fluctuation in demand before the next order is placed is unimportant. This is because any increase in demand will simply mean that an order is placed earlier than expected. However once an order has been placed any increase in demand is more serious and could result in a stock-out. To prevent this happening a buffer (or safety) stock is purchased. The stock level diagram now looks like Figure 5 below.

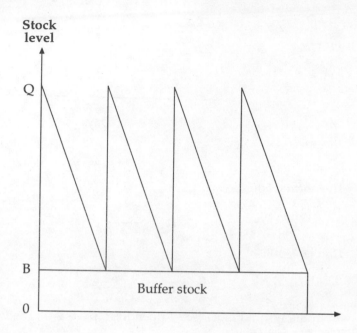

Figure 5

It is now a matter of calculating the size (B) of the buffer stock. However, before this can be done an assumption needs to be made regarding the distribution of demand. The simplest assumption is to say that the demand is normally distributed. The use of the normal distribution means that it is possible for the demand to reach very high levels since the tails of the distribution in theory have no end. However in practise a limit is set such as 5% and the demand is found that is only exceeded for this percentage of times.

Activity 5

The demand for the game 'Aliens' is normally distributed with a mean of 16.7 games per day and a standard deviation of 5.2 games. What buffer level should be maintained such that there is less than a 5% chance of running out of stock during the lead time of 4 days? What extra cost does this incur?

During the 4 days lead time the mean demand will be $4 \times 16.7 = 66.8$ games. Calculation of the standard deviation for the 4 days can be found using the formula:

$$\sqrt{n \times \sigma^2}$$

Where n is the lead time and σ is the standard deviation per unit time period. The standard deviation is therefore:

$$\sqrt{4 \times 5.2^2} = 10.4$$

The demand that is exceeded on only 5% of occasions is denoted by X in Figure 6 below.

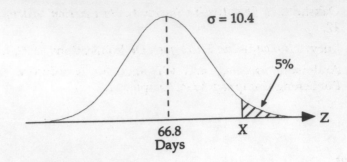

Figure 6

The normal equation is:

$$Z = \frac{X - \mu}{\sigma}$$

That is:

$$Z = \frac{X - 66.8}{10.4}$$

From the normal table (see Appendix 2, page 110), the value of Z for a probability of 0.05 (5%) is 1.645 so:

$$1.645 = \frac{X - 66.8}{10.4}$$

That is:

$$1.645 \times 10.4 = X - 66.8$$

$$17.108 = X - 66.8$$

and

$$X = 17.108 + 66.8$$

$$= 83.9$$

This means that on 5% of occasions the demand could exceed 83.9 units. The buffer level to ensure that a stock-out only occurs on 5% of occasions is 83.9 − 66.8 = 17.1 units (say 18 units). In practise this would be rounded up to 20 or even more. To ensure that this buffer stock is maintained at the correct level the re-order level will need to be set at 84 units (The rounded value of 'X').

The additional storage cost will be 18 × the holding cost, that is 18 × 10 = £180 p.a. since 18 units are permanently in stock.

6.6 Summary

This chapter has introduced you to some methods employed in reducing the costs of holding stock. The EOQ model makes the assumption that the demand for a product is known and constant. If this is approximately true the re-order quantity is that quantity that minimises the sum of the ordering and holding costs. Frequently it is cheaper to buy larger quantities than that specified by the EOQ formula as a discount may be given for large orders. Although it is assumed that the demand is constant it is possible to relax this assumption somewhat by employing a buffer or safety stock. This buffer stock can be calculated if the demand for the product is assumed to be normally distributed.

6.7 Further reading

Morris, C, *Quantitative Approaches in Business Studies*, Pitman, 1993, Chapter 15

Oakshott, L, *Quantitative Approaches to Decision Making*, DP Publications, 1993, Unit 17.

Lucy, T, *Quantitative Techniques*, DP Publications, 1992, Chapters 11 to 14.

Anderson, Sweeney and Williams, *An Introduction to Management Science*, West Publishing Company, 1994, Chapter 11.

6.8 Exercises

Progress questions

These question have been designed to help you remember the key points in this chapter. The answers to these questions are given in Appendix 1, page 109.

Give the missing word in each case:

1. Stock holding costs can be divided into two broad categories. These are storage costs and .... costs.

2. EOQ stands for the Economic .... quantity model.

3. The EOQ model is an example of a .... model.

4. The EOQ model assumes that demand is known and ....

5. In order to take discounts into account, the .... cost must also be known.

6. A .... stock is required to ensure that stockouts do not occur.

Answer TRUE or FALSE

7. At minimum cost the order cost equals the holding cost.

    True ☐ False ☐

8. The product cost does not form part of the EOQ formula.

    True ☐ False ☐

9. You do not need to know the product cost for deciding whether to take advantage of quantity discounts.

    True ☐ False ☐

10. A buffer stock will guarantee that you never have a stock-out.

    True ☐ False ☐

Review questions

These questions have been designed to help you check your comprehension of the key points in this chapter. You may wish to look further than this chapter in order to answer them fully. You will find the reading list useful in this respect. You can check the essential elements of your answers by referring to the appropriate section.

11. What stock related costs are likely to be incurred by a fresh food distributor. (Section 6.2)

12. What are the assumptions of the EOQ model. (Section 6.3)

13. When might it be useful to consider discounts? (Section 6.2)

Multiple choice questions

The answers to these will be given in the Lecturers' Supplement.

14. If the order cost is £10 per order then the total order cost if 5 orders are made per year is:
    A. £10
    B. £50
    C. £15

15. The minimum total costs occur when:
    A. The order cost and holding cost are equal.
    B. The order cost is at a minimum.
    C. The holding cost is at a minimum.

16. If the cost of holding stock is £5 per unit p.a then the holding cost per annum for an order quantity of 100 is:
    A. £500
    B. £5
    C. £250

17. If a buffer stock is used it is necessary to assume that the demand during the lead time is:
    A. Constant
    B. Normally distributed
    C. known

18. If standard deviation of demand is 5 units per week then the standard deviation during the lead time of 3 weeks is:
    A. 15
    B. 8.66
    C. 75

19. A buffer stock of 200 units is held. If the cost of holding one unit in stock for a year is £5, the holding cost (p.a) of the buffer stock will be:
    A. £1000
    B. £500
    C. £5

Practice questions

Answers to these questions will be given in the Lecturers' Supplement.

20. The annual demand for a product is 4800 units, each unit costs £70 each for orders less than 600 and £68 each for orders of 600 or more. If an order costs £9 to set up and the annual stock holding costs are 20% of the average value of stock held, determine the optimum stock ordering policy. What is the cost of this policy?

21. The demand for a particular product is normally distributed with a mean of 100 units per day and a standard deviation of 20 units. If the lead time is 5 days, determine the buffer stock level such that there is less than a 5% chance of running out of stock.

22. A depot receives petrol from a refinery, which insists on a minimum of 3 days notice for deliveries. The minimum delivery quantity is a road tanker load which is 20,000 gallons. The depot is charged £570 for a delivery, regardless of the number of tankers used.

    If the cost of storage of the petrol is estimated to be 1p per gallon per day, what is the best ordering policy for the depot? (i.e. order quantity, average time between orders and the quantity of petrol in stock which triggers a new order). What is the cost of this policy?

23. A paint shop uses 200 tins of paint per day at a fairly constant rate. Tins are now ordered in batches of 1000 when the stock drops below 500. Delivery time is one day. The cost of placing an order is £100. Holding costs are 25p per tin per day.

    a) You have been asked to examine this policy and make any suitable recommendations to reduce costs.

    b) The supplier is offering a bulk order discount of 2% off the selling price of £10 for orders above 2000 tins. Advise whether or not they should take up the offer.

    c) What is the minimum percentage discount the shop ought to consider to make it worthwhile to order in quantities of 2000?

Assignment

Answers to this assignment are included in the Lecturers' supplement.

Riglen plc cooks and cans food products for sale in its supermarkets. It uses 500,000 medium size cans per annum at a fairly uniform rate, which it purchases from the Tin Can company. Tin Can charge £100 per 5000 cans plus a delivery charge of £50 regardless of the size of the order. Riglen's current order policy is to order 10,000 cans every week but during a cost auditing exercise the canning department has been criticised for such frequent ordering. As a consequence of this criticism, Jeff Lea, the Canning Production Manager has been told to review the department's ordering policy.

Jeff has asked you to help him cost out the current system and to help you have told that it was costs the company 1.5p p.a to hold one can in stock. (This 1.5p is made up of interests charges and cost of storage facilities).

a) What is the average quantity of stock currently held? and how much does this cost the company each year in holding costs?

b) How many orders are made each year and what does this cost the company? (Assume that the company works for 50 weeks a year).

c) What is the sum of these two costs?

d) Use the EOQ formula to calculate the best order quantity. What is the saving in cost if this order quantity was used rather than the current order of 10,000. What is the time between orders with your calculated order quantity?

e) You have now been asked to consider increasing the order quantity to 100,000, as at this quantity the price is reduced to £99 per 5000 cans. Is it worth ordering this larger quantity?

f) The weekly demand for cans is not constant but is normally distributed with an average of 10,000 cans and a standard deviation of 5,000 cans. What re-order level would be required to ensure that the probability of a stock-out is less than 1%?

7 Simulation

7.1 Introduction

The quantitative techniques that you have met so far have allowed analytical solutions to problems to be found. For example the inventory control (EOQ) model is a simple formula that will enable you to calculate the order quantity that will minimise inventory costs. (See Chapter 6 page 84). These techniques or models are called deterministic because it is assumed that the variables are known precisely. However, there is another model class called stochastic. A stochastic model has at least one variable that does not have a single value – it has many possible values defined by some probability distribution. A Queueing system is an example of a stochastic model and even relatively simple queueing models are difficult to solve analytically. This chapter looks at the use of simulation to solve simple queueing models.

On completing this chapter you should be able to:

❑ Appreciate the reasons for using simulation to solve stochastic models.

❑ Understand the differences between terminating and non-terminating systems.

❑ Demonstrate the technique of simulation by using the tabular method for simple problems.

7.2 Queueing problems

There are many instances of queueing situations. Whenever you go to the supermarket or the bank you will inevitably have to join a queue to be served. Why is this? The reason is that the arrival of customers to a service facility is unpredictable. Although you may know that 30 people an hour will arrive to be served you cannot predict when they will arrive. You may get 10 people in the first 5 minutes then no one for another 10 minutes. This is just like tossing a coin 10 times; although you may expect 5 heads and 5 tails, you wouldn't be that surprised to get 7 heads or even 10 heads. And just like tossing the coin the average of 30 people an hour will be achieved over a long period of time but in the short term unpredictable results can happen. This unpredictable behaviour means that it is very difficult to avoid queues. You could increase the capacity of the service facility but you would then find that this expensive resource is lying idle much of the time. The solution of queueing problem is therefore a compromise between having excessive queues and an under-utilised resource.

Some simple queueing problems can be solved analytically but the vast majority have to be solved using a technique called simulation. The following example illustrates a typical queueing problem.

Example

Passengers arriving at a suburban rail ticket office during the morning peak commuter period frequently have to wait for service. There is one clerk who issues tickets and provides an information service for passengers. The manager has received complaints regarding the time passengers spend in the queue waiting to be served and she wishes to investigate possible methods of reducing the queueing time. Possible ideas include employing a second ticket clerk who could either duplicate the existing clerk or perhaps handle enquiries only. Another idea may be to collect fares on the train. The manager decided to collect data on arrivals and service times over a number of days and the final figures have been summarised in the following tables:

Table 1

Inter-arrival time (secs)	Frequency (%)
0 to under 30	55
30 to under 60	30
60 to under 90	10
90 to under 120	5

Table 2

Service time (secs)	frequency (%)
20 to under 30	17
30 to under 40	28
40 to under 50	25
50 to under 60	20
60 to under 90	10

Activity 1

Describe the components of the queueing system inherent in this example.

You probably realise that passengers must first arrive and then either join a queue or go straight to be served. Once served, passengers leave the 'system'. This can be better described by the means of a diagram.

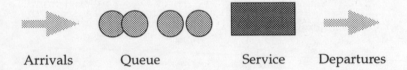

Arrivals   Queue   Service   Departures

Figure 1 Ticket office system

Activity 2

The manager has a few ideas for reducing the queues. Why shouldn't she just try them out and see which is the best?

This method is probably done in many cases but it can be costly and may disrupt the entire system if you are not careful. In some cases experimenting with the real system can be dangerous. For example, trying out changes to the safety devices of a nuclear power station is not recommended! Developing a model of a system and experimenting on this is much cheaper, safer and less disruptive. Of course the model needs to be accurate and much time is spent by analysts validating their model. A model can only be an approximation of the real system and the validation checks will tell you how close your model is to the real system. You may for instance not have allowed for the fact that passengers 'balk' from a queue, that is do not wait to be served. If this is important it can be included and the model re-validated.

7.3 Random numbers

Although you may be sure that 30 customers turn up to be served every hour you cannot be sure when during that hour they will arrive. You may get 10 people in the first minute and then no-one turns up for the next 15 minutes. In other words there is a randomness in the way customers are likely to arrive. This randomness is apparent in most systems and is the reason why deterministic models are not very good at solving real problems. In order for simulation to take this randomness into account, random numbers are used.

True random numbers can only be generated by physical devices such as a roulette wheel which ensures that the distribution is uniform, that is each number has an equal chance of being picked. In addition the sequence of numbers so produced is non-repeatable. However most simulations are carried out on a computer and the random numbers in this case are generated by a formula within the computer. Although the random numbers produced are not true random numbers they behave like true random numbers and are called pseudo random numbers. The table of random numbers included in Appendix 2, page 113 were generated by a computer and are therefore pseudo random numbers.

The purpose of random numbers is to allow you (or the computer) to randomly select an arrival or service time from the appropriate distribution. The frequency tables given in the example represent the distribution of arrival time and service time for the ticket office. Random numbers can be arranged in any order and for this case two digit numbers would match the percentage format in the tables. If you look at this table you will see that 55% of inter-arrival times are in the range 0 to under 30 seconds. The random numbers 00 to 54 (or 01 to 55) could therefore be used to represent this time band.

Activity 3

The next time band in table 1 is 30 to under 60 seconds. What random numbers would you use to represent this band? Repeat this procedure for the last two bands.

Since the frequency is 30% the random numbers should be 55 to 84 (or 56 to 85) inclusive. For the last two bands the random numbers should be 85 to 94 (86 to 95) and 95 to 99 (96 to 00) inclusive.

If a computer package was used to simulate this system then a routine within the program would generate a random number and then obtain the appropriate inter-arrival time by interpolation.

For example if the random number 15 was generated then the inter-arrival time would be 8.2 seconds ($\frac{15}{55}$ of 30).

However when manually carrying out a simulation it is much easier to represent each time band by its mid point, so any random number between 00 to 54 would correspond to an inter-arrival time of 15 seconds. This can be repeated for all bands and to do this you may find it easier to write down the cumulative frequencies as in the modified table below.

Inter-arrival time mid point	Frequency (%)	Cumulative frequency	Random numbers
15	55	55	00 – 54
45	30	85	55 – 84
75	10	95	85 – 94
105	5	100	95 – 99

The table you should have obtained is shown below:

Service mid point	Frequency	Cumulative frequency	Random numbers
25	17	17	00 – 16
35	28	45	17 – 44
45	25	70	45 – 69
55	20	90	70 – 89
75	10	100	90 – 99

Again a particular service time would be represented by a range of random numbers. For example, a service time of 55 seconds would be represented by the random numbers 70 to 89.

7.4 Tabular simulation

The easiest method of demonstrating simulation is by manually simulating a simple system. In order to carry out the simulation of the ticket office manually you would need to obtain a stream of random numbers. These can conveniently be obtained from tables (see Appendix 2, page 113). These numbers would then be used to sample from the arrival and service time distributions. For example, suppose that the first few random numbers are 08, 72, 87 and 46. The random number 08 represents an inter-arrival time of 15 seconds so the first passenger arrives at a clock time 15. There is no queue so this passenger can be served immediately. The random number 72 corresponds to a service time of 55 seconds so this service will end at a clock time of 70 (15 + 55). The next customer arrives 75 seconds after the first so the clock time of 90 is after the end of the last service. The second passenger can also be served immediately. The service time is 45 seconds so the passenger departs at 135. This information is best displayed in tabular format similar to the one below:

RNo	Inter-arr.	Clock time	RNo	Service time	Starts	Ends	Waiting time
08	15	15	72	55	15	70	0
87	75	90	46	45	90	135	0

The last column of this table allows the waiting time of each passenger to be recorded.

The table you should have ended up with is shown below:

RNo	Inter-arr.	Clock time	RNo	Service time	Starts	Ends	Waiting time
08	15	15	72	55	15	70	0
87	75	90	46	45	90	135	0
15	15	105	96	75	135	210	30
04	15	120	00	25	210	235	90
52	15	135	27	35	235	270	100
46	15	150	73	55	270	325	120
95	105	255	76	55	325	380	70
10	15	270	25	35	380	415	110
02	15	285	11	25	415	440	130

As you can see the calculations are not difficult but they are tedious and time consuming.

Activity 6

What is the average waiting time for the simulation above?

The average waiting time of the first 9 passenger is 72.2 seconds but it appears that the waiting time is increasing as the simulation proceeds.

7.5 Accuracy of simulation results

To obtain reliable results the simulation of the ticket office would need to be continued for the duration of the morning rush hour (say 2 hours or 7200 seconds) and more than one run would be necessary.

Activity 7

Why should multiple runs of a simulation be necessary?

The reason for multiple runs is partly to do with the variability that you will get using random numbers and partly to aid statistical analysis. One run of a simulation uses a stream of random numbers and different streams could give quite different results. There is nothing wrong with this – the variations are reflecting the situations that occur in real life. In fact you can think of simulation as a sampling device. Each run of the simulation generates estimates of the performance of the system, such as the mean waiting time. If you want to carry out statistical analysis on your results, such as obtaining a confidence interval of the true mean waiting time, you will need values obtained from several runs.

The method of replicating the simulation run depends on whether the system is a terminating one or non-terminating. A terminating system is, as its name suggests, a system that stops after a certain time or after a certain number of entities (customers) have passed through the system.

Activity 8

Is the ticket office example a terminating or non-terminating system?

In busy main line terminals you could argue that the ticket office doesn't shut so the system must be non-terminating. However, in this example it is only the morning peak period that you are interested in so for practical purposes this is a terminating system.

For terminating systems the length of the simulation is fixed and this can simply be repeated a number of times using a different random number stream each time. This is called the method of independent replications.

Non-terminating systems do not have any natural end and could be considered to continue indefinitely. Examples include airports, harbours, 24 hour casualty departments and many production processes. Although some artificial end could be assumed and the independent replications method used, it is usual to use the batch means method. This method makes one very long run of the simulation but is halted at regular intervals. At the end of each interval the average performance measure during the interval is noted. The reason that this method is preferred is to do with initial bias. This is the bias caused by assuming the all queues are empty at the start of the simulation.

Most terminating systems start in the empty state so initial bias is not a problem in this case. However with non-terminating systems it is a problem and it is necessary for the system to reach steady state before results are collected. A system is in steady state if its current state is independent of the starting conditions. The length of time necessary for a system to reach steady state can only be found by experimentation.

If the method of independent replications was used for non-terminating systems, steady state would need to be reached for each run which is wasteful even with fast computers. With the batch means method, steady state only needs to be found once. Results from the period following steady state only are used in the analysis of the system. Figure 2 below illustrates the two methods.

Method of independent replications

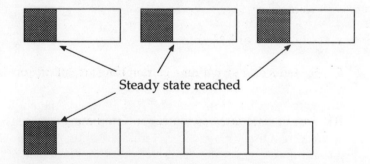

Batch means method

Figure 2 Methods of replicating runs of a simulation

7.6 Summary

Simulation is a very popular and useful technique for solving problems that cannot be solved using more conventional methods. This is particularly true for complex queueing systems. Random numbers form the heart of a simulation and mimic the variability that occurs in the real system. Systems can be of two types; terminating and non-terminating. Terminating systems are systems that have a fixed start and end and multiple runs of a terminating model can be achieved using the method of independent replications. Non-terminating systems are not so easy to analyse because the start of a simulation assumes empty queues, which is unrealistic. The time for a non-terminating system to reach steady state must be found and then multiple runs made using the batch means method.

7.7 Further reading

Morris, C, *Quantitative Approaches in Business Studies*, Pitman, 1993, Chapter 18.

Oakshott, L, *Quantitative Approaches to Decision Making*, DP Publications, 1993, Unit 20.

Pidd, M, *Computer Simulation in Management Science*, Wiley, 1992, Chapters 1,2,3 and 7.

7.8 Exercises

Progress questions

These question have been designed to help you remember the key points in this chapter. The answers to these questions are given in Appendix 1, page 109.

Give the missing word in each case:

1. Simulation is normally used to solve complex .... models.

2. Simulation avoids experimenting on the real ....

3. Random numbers are used to reproduce the .... that is inherent in most systems

4. A stream of true random numbers is not ....

5. Random numbers produced by a formula are called .... random numbers.

6. Simulations need to be .... against the real system to ensure that they produce accurate results.

Answer TRUE or FALSE

7. Systems that stop after a certain time are called terminating systems.

    True ☐ False ☐

8. Steady state must be found for terminating systems.

    True ☐ False ☐

9. In a terminating systems all queues start in the empty state.

    True ☐ False ☐

10. Only one run of a terminating system is required.

    True ☐ False ☐

11. The method of replicating runs of a non-terminating system is called the batch means method.

    True ☐ False ☐

Review questions

> *These questions have been designed to help you check your comprehension of the key points in this chapter. You may wish to look further than this chapter in order to answer them fully. You will find the reading list useful in this respect. You can check the essential elements of your answers by referring to the appropriate section.*

12. Explain why averages are of no help in analysing a stochastic system. (Sections 7.2 and 7.3)

13. What are the components of a queueing system? (Section 7.2)

14. Describe the essential differences between a terminating and non-terminating system. (Section 7.5)

Multiple choice questions

> *The answers to these will be given in the Lecturers' Supplement.*

15. A queueing system is an example of a:
    A. Deterministic system
    B. Stochastic system
    C. Dynamic system

16. Pseudo random numbers are random numbers that:
    A. Can be repeated
    B. Cannot be repeated
    C. Are biased

17. A bank is an example of:
    A. A terminating system
    B. A non-terminating system
    C. Neither

18. A simulation model needs to be run:
    A. Once only
    B. Twice
    C. At least 10 times

Practice questions

> *Answers to these questions will be given in the Lecturers' Supplement.*

19. Customers arrive at a single cash dispenser with the following inter-arrival time distribution:

Inter-arrival time (secs)	% Frequency
20 to under 50	5
50 to under 100	20
100 to under 150	30
150 to under 200	45

The service time is 45 seconds.

Using the random numbers below, manually simulate the system and find the average time spent waiting for service and the utilisation of the cash dispenser.

08, 72, 87, 46, 75, 73, 00, 11, 27, 07, 05, 20, 30, 85, 22, 21, 04, 67, 19, 13

20. Customers arrive at a bank, which has only a single cashier, with the inter-arrival time and service time distributions shown below.

Inter-arrival time (minutes)	% of customers	Service time (minutes)	% of customers
0 to under 4	30	0 to under 1	0
4 to under 6	40	1 to under 3	50
6 to under 8	20	3 to under 5	40
8 to under 10	10	5 to under 7	10

Using the random numbers given below, simulate the next 6 arrivals and find the mean time that they spend queueing for the cashier.

04, 10, 59, 07, 38, 98, 01, 75, 48, 91, 04, 12

21. Ajax Food Products has its main factory in the centre of Bristol. Lorries arrive at a constant rate from 08.00 to 18.00 five days a week where they are either loaded or unloaded using the single loading/unloading bay and on a first come first served basis. The area around the factory is frequently congested with lorries because the loading/unloading depot is not large enough for all arriving lorries to wait. A suggestion has been made that an improvement in numbers queueing times might result if priority was given to lorries that required unloading. This is because unloading is generally a faster operation. However before any decision is made it has been decided to build a simulation model of the current system.

a. Briefly discuss the advantages and disadvantages of simulation as a means of experimenting on this system.

b. Using the random numbers 42, 17, 38 and 61, demonstrate how four unloading times could be generated from the frequency distribution given below.

Unloading times

Time (minutes)	% frequency
0 to under 30	20
30 to under 40	35
40 to under 50	22
50 to under 60	15
60 to under 70	8

Assignment

Answers to this assignment are included in the Lecturers' supplement.

Andrew Giles the Transport manager at Bristol Tyres has just returned from a meeting with the Managing Director. Apparently the police have received complaints from local residents about the parking of heavy lorries in the side streets near the factory. This is occurring because there is insufficient room in the depot for lorries to wait to be loaded/unloaded.

To reduce the congestion it has been suggested a second bay be built. However, before this is done a simulation of the current system is to be developed and you been asked to take on this project.

Your first task was a data collection exercise and this gave you the following information.

i)   The depot is open from 0800 to 1800 Mondays to Fridays.

ii)   Vehicles either require loading or unloading (not both)

iii) 70% of lorries require loading and 30% unloading.

iv)   The frequency distributions of the loading/unloading operations found by timing a large number of lorries was as follows.

Time (minutes)	Loading % frequency	Unloading % frequency
0 to under 30	20	30
30 to under 40	35	40
40 to under 50	22	25
50 to under 60	15	4
60 to under 70	8	1

v)   The frequency distribution of the inter-arrival time, that is the time between successive arrivals was as follows.

Time (minutes)	% frequency
0 to under 10	15
10 to under 20	40
20 to under 30	30
30 to under 40	5
40 to under 50	5
50 to under 60	3
60 to under 70	2

You have also made the following assumptions:

i)   The pattern of arrivals is constant throughout the day.

ii)   A second bay would be used like the first, that is for loading and unloading.

iii) A single queue of lorries would form and a lorry could use either bay on a 'first come, first served basis'.

iv)   Any lorries in the queue at the end of the day would be loaded or unloaded.

Assignment (continued)

a) Explain why simulation is a better method than simulating on the real system for this problem.

b) How would you go about simulating the system? In your answer you should discuss the run length of the simulation and the number of runs required.

c) Demonstrate the technique of simulation by using the tabular method to simulate three hours (180 minutes) of depot operation. What is the average waiting time of the lorries?

Random numbers:

20, 17, 42, 96, 23, 17, 28, 66, 38, 59, 38, 61,

73, 76, 80, 00, 20, 56, 10, 05, 87, 88, 78, 15

d) Repeat the simulation using 2 unloading bays.

Appendices

Chapter 6 Inventory control

1. Order	2. Order	3. Deterministic	4. Constant
5. Product	6. Buffer (or safety)	7. True	8. True
9. False	10. False		

Chapter 7 Simulation

1. Stochastic	2. System	3. Variability	4. Repeatable
5. Pseudo	6. Validated	7. True	8. False
9. True	10. False	11. True	

Appendix 2 Statistical tables

Areas in the right hand tail of the standard normal distribution

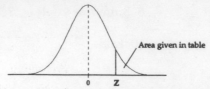

Z	0.00	0.01	0.02	0.03	0.04	0.05	0.06	0.07	0.08	0.09
0.0	0.5000	0.4960	0.4920	0.4880	0.4840	0.4801	0.4761	0.4721	0.4681	0.4641
0.1	0.4602	0.4562	0.4522	0.4483	0.4443	0.4404	0.4364	0.4325	0.4286	0.4247
0.2	0.4207	0.4168	0.4129	0.4090	0.4052	0.4013	0.3974	0.3936	0.3897	0.3859
0.3	0.3821	0.3783	0.3745	0.3707	0.3669	0.3632	0.3594	0.3557	0.3520	0.3483
0.4	0.3446	0.3409	0.3372	0.3336	0.3300	0.3264	0.3228	0.3192	0.3156	0.3121
0.5	0.3085	0.3050	0.3015	0.2981	0.2946	0.2912	0.2877	0.2843	0.2810	0.2776
0.6	0.2743	0.2709	0.2676	0.2643	0.2611	0.2578	0.2546	0.2514	0.2483	0.2451
0.7	0.2420	0.2389	0.2358	0.2327	0.2296	0.2266	0.2236	0.2206	0.2177	0.2148
0.8	0.2119	0.2090	0.2061	0.2033	0.2005	0.1977	0.1949	0.1922	0.1894	0.1867
0.9	0.1841	0.1814	0.1788	0.1762	0.1736	0.1711	0.1685	0.1660	0.1635	0.1611
1.0	0.1587	0.1562	0.1539	0.1515	0.1492	0.1469	0.1446	0.1423	0.1401	0.1379
1.1	0.1357	0.1335	0.1314	0.1292	0.1271	0.1251	0.1230	0.1210	0.1190	0.1170
1.2	0.1151	0.1131	0.1112	0.1093	0.1075	0.1056	0.1038	0.1020	0.1003	0.0985
1.3	0.0968	0.0951	0.0934	0.0918	0.0901	0.0885	0.0869	0.0853	0.0838	0.0823
1.4	0.0808	0.0793	0.0778	0.0764	0.0749	0.0735	0.0721	0.0708	0.0694	0.0681
1.5	0.0668	0.0655	0.0643	0.0630	0.0618	0.0606	0.0594	0.0582	0.0571	0.0559
1.6	0.0548	0.0537	0.0526	0.0516	0.0505	0.0495	0.0485	0.0475	0.0465	0.0455
1.7	0.0446	0.0436	0.0427	0.0418	0.0409	0.0401	0.0392	0.0384	0.0375	0.0367
1.8	0.0359	0.0351	0.0344	0.0336	0.0329	0.0322	0.0314	0.0307	0.0301	0.0294
1.9	0.0287	0.0281	0.0274	0.0268	0.0262	0.0256	0.0250	0.0244	0.0239	0.0233
2.0	0.0228	0.0222	0.0217	0.0212	0.0207	0.0202	0.0197	0.0192	0.0188	0.0183
2.1	0.0179	0.0174	0.0170	0.0166	0.0162	0.0158	0.0154	0.0150	0.0146	0.0143
2.2	0.0139	0.0136	0.0132	0.0129	0.0125	0.0122	0.0119	0.0116	0.0113	0.0110
2.3	0.0107	0.0104	0.0102	0.0099	0.0096	0.0094	0.0091	0.0089	0.0087	0.0084
2.4	0.0082	0.0080	0.0078	0.0075	0.0073	0.0071	0.0069	0.0068	0.0066	0.0064
2.5	0.0062	0.0060	0.0059	0.0057	0.0055	0.0054	0.0052	0.0051	0.0049	0.0048
2.6	0.0047	0.0045	0.0044	0.0043	0.0041	0.0040	0.0039	0.0038	0.0037	0.0036
2.7	0.0035	0.0034	0.0033	0.0032	0.0031	0.0030	0.0029	0.0028	0.0027	0.0026
2.8	0.0026	0.0025	0.0024	0.0023	0.0023	0.0022	0.0021	0.0021	0.0020	0.0019
2.9	0.0019	0.0018	0.0018	0.0017	0.0016	0.0016	0.0015	0.0015	0.0014	0.0014

3.0 0.0013   3.1 0.0010   3.2 0.0007   3.3 0.0005   3.4 0.0003

Table of the t-distribution

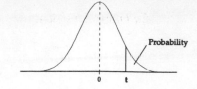

Probability

df	0.2	0.1	0.05	0.025	0.01	0.005	0.001	0.0001
1	1.376	3.078	6.314	12.706	31.821	63.657	318.309	3183.1
2	1.061	1.886	2.920	4.303	6.965	9.925	22.327	70.700
3	0.978	1.638	2.353	3.182	4.541	5.841	10.215	22.204
4	0.941	1.533	2.132	2.776	3.747	4.604	7.173	13.034
5	0.920	1.476	2.015	2.571	3.365	4.032	5.893	9.678
6	0.906	1.440	1.943	2.447	3.143	3.707	5.208	8.025
7	0.896	1.415	1.895	2.365	2.998	3.499	4.785	7.063
8	0.889	1.397	1.860	2.306	2.896	3.355	4.501	6.442
9	0.883	1.383	1.833	2.262	2.821	3.250	4.297	6.010
10	0.879	1.372	1.812	2.228	2.764	3.169	4.144	5.694
11	0.876	1.363	1.796	2.201	2.718	3.106	4.025	5.453
12	0.873	1.356	1.782	2.179	2.681	3.055	3.930	5.263
13	0.870	1.350	1.771	2.160	2.650	3.012	3.852	5.111
14	0.868	1.345	1.761	2.145	2.624	2.977	3.787	4.985
15	0.866	1.341	1.753	2.131	2.602	2.947	3.733	4.880
16	0.865	1.337	1.746	2.120	2.583	2.921	3.686	4.791
17	0.863	1.333	1.740	2.110	2.567	2.898	3.646	4.714
18	0.862	1.330	1.734	2.101	2.552	2.878	3.610	4.648
19	0.861	1.328	1.729	2.093	2.539	2.861	3.579	4.590
20	0.860	1.325	1.725	2.086	2.528	2.845	3.552	4.539
21	0.859	1.323	1.721	2.080	2.518	2.831	3.527	4.493
22	0.858	1.321	1.717	2.074	2.508	2.819	3.505	4.452
23	0.858	1.319	1.714	2.069	2.500	2.807	3.485	4.415
24	0.857	1.318	1.711	2.064	2.492	2.797	3.467	4.382
25	0.856	1.316	1.708	2.060	2.485	2.787	3.450	4.352
26	0.856	1.315	1.706	2.056	2.479	2.779	3.435	4.324
27	0.855	1.314	1.703	2.052	2.473	2.771	3.421	4.299
28	0.855	1.313	1.701	2.048	2.467	2.763	3.408	4.275
29	0.854	1.311	1.699	2.045	2.462	2.756	3.396	4.254
30	0.854	1.310	1.697	2.042	2.457	2.750	3.385	4.234
35	0.852	1.306	1.690	2.030	2.438	2.724	3.340	4.153
40	0.851	1.303	1.684	2.021	2.423	2.704	3.307	4.094
45	0.850	1.301	1.679	2.014	2.412	2.690	3.281	4.049
50	0.849	1.299	1.676	2.009	2.403	2.678	3.261	4.014
60	0.848	1.296	1.671	2.000	2.390	2.660	3.232	3.962
80	0.846	1.292	1.664	1.990	2.374	2.639	3.195	3.899
100	0.845	1.290	1.660	1.984	2.364	2.626	3.174	3.862
∞	0.842	1.282	1.645	1.960	2.327	2.576	3.091	3.720

Table of the X² distibution

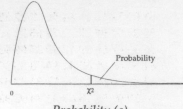

Probability

0   X²

Probability (a)

df	0.995	0.99	0.9	0.1	0.05	0.025	0.01	0.005	0.001
1	0.000	0.000	0.016	2.706	3.841	5.024	6.635	7.879	10.828
2	0.010	0.020	0.211	4.605	5.991	7.378	9.210	10.597	13.816
3	0.072	0.115	0.584	6.251	7.815	9.348	11.345	12.838	16.266
4	0.207	0.297	1.064	7.779	9.488	11.143	13.277	14.860	18.467
5	0.412	0.554	1.610	9.236	11.070	12.833	15.086	16.750	20.515
6	0.676	0.872	2.204	10.645	12.592	14.449	16.812	18.548	22.458
7	0.989	1.239	2.833	12.017	14.067	16.013	18.475	20.278	24.322
8	1.344	1.646	3.490	13.362	15.507	17.535	20.090	21.955	26.124
9	1.735	2.088	4.168	14.684	16.919	19.023	21.666	23.589	27.877
10	2.156	2.558	4.865	15.987	18.307	20.483	23.209	25.188	29.588
11	2.603	3.053	5.578	17.275	19.675	21.920	24.725	26.757	31.264
12	3.074	3.571	6.304	18.549	21.026	23.337	26.217	28.300	32.909
13	3.565	4.107	7.042	19.812	22.362	24.736	27.688	29.819	34.528
14	4.075	4.660	7.790	21.064	23.685	26.119	29.141	31.319	36.123
15	4.601	5.229	8.547	22.307	24.996	27.488	30.578	32.801	37.697
16	5.142	5.812	9.312	23.542	26.296	28.845	32.000	34.267	39.252
17	5.697	6.408	10.085	24.769	27.587	30.191	33.409	35.718	40.790
18	6.265	7.015	10.865	25.989	28.869	31.526	34.805	37.156	42.312
19	6.844	7.633	11.651	27.204	30.144	32.852	36.191	38.582	43.820
20	7.434	8.260	12.443	28.412	31.410	34.170	37.566	39.997	45.315
21	8.034	8.897	13.240	29.615	32.671	35.479	38.932	41.401	46.797
22	8.643	9.542	14.041	30.813	33.924	36.781	40.289	42.796	48.268
23	9.260	10.196	14.848	32.007	35.172	38.076	41.638	44.181	49.728
24	9.886	10.856	15.659	33.196	36.415	39.364	42.980	45.559	51.179
25	0.520	11.524	16.473	34.382	37.652	40.646	44.314	46.928	52.620
26	1.160	12.198	17.292	35.563	38.885	41.923	45.642	48.290	54.052
27	1.808	12.879	18.114	36.741	40.113	43.195	46.963	49.645	55.476
28	2.461	13.565	18.939	37.916	41.337	44.461	48.278	50.993	56.892
29	3.121	14.256	19.768	39.087	42.557	45.722	49.588	52.336	58.301
30	3.787	14.953	20.599	40.256	43.773	46.979	50.892	53.672	59.703
35	7.192	18.509	24.797	46.059	49.802	53.203	57.342	60.275	66.619
40	0.707	22.164	29.051	51.805	55.758	59.342	63.691	66.766	73.402

Random Numbers

```
61 05 72 60 15 64 56 12 22 75 67 50
93 35 01 96 17 22 79 65 21 30 35 32
66 86 67 59 39 17 95 35 09 93 55 84
81 60 69 99 62 41 84 78 35 30 48 75
07 30 30 84 23 98 71 73 47 67 42 68
93 30 94 55 18 69 88 33 95 92 45 58
46 60 25 98 75 93 24 74 46 61 46 64
23 35 12 21 19 30 63 88 62 20 20 36
41 10 18 14 96 67 64 62 69 53 22 76
72 63 52 74 07 25 79 75 39 37 58 00
87 67 39 51 97 06 98 76 37 96 32 70
99 75 90 53 12 65 17 68 37 69 97 81
67 48 83 85 54 95 31 21 41 93 35 79
77 94 94 49 11 52 22 83 44 52 20 92
22 99 75 45 36 36 64 39 52 18 67 41
20 04 39 20 52 08 20 06 33 33 95 80
61 81 91 67 09 04 55 52 24 20 75 88
25 86 83 87 37 13 95 19 20 16 05 69
92 42 73 97 76 74 69 34 90 19 27 84
14 82 43 69 03 29 35 50 70 19 97 51
61 56 52 18 48 03 34 74 16 13 27 15
40 20 59 51 95 88 03 21 18 80 98 72
01 42 80 72 50 39 76 45 01 38 13 02
93 62 01 12 63 79 90 36 75 71 25 80
80 00 21 32 91 48 60 82 08 84 41 53
13 89 58 15 34 28 81 93 07 12 19 39
40 98 25 11 73 48 51 86 92 35 37 20
52 47 37 87 30 81 64 80 32 09 50 09
33 38 64 75 77 79 13 73 48 54 56 52
32 74 76 66 95 81 11 87 04 46 55 56
68 07 20 57 47 14 53 32 32 01 94 19
57 11 99 88 82 88 05 44 35 13 51 79
73 21 75 54 84 11 38 67 42 38 68 99
51 23 07 05 60 78 51 10 03 53 03 49
98 93 98 48 04 02 78 77 76 67 69 29
58 89 74 64 41 12 31 16 76 43 70 52
62 11 34 91 54 04 74 03 40 78 15 56
47 97 51 85 80 15 26 42 85 72 94 08
97 33 80 82 62 74 29 87 77 43 94 09
41 23 26 40 87 64 59 78 34 72 60 69
69 54 08 18 60 12 00 92 62 21 48 47
09 47 49 69 18 68 20 79 42 36 48 28
81 95 35 72 19 28 05 47 18 40 61 79
10 81 27 04 57 82 60 71 47 35 93 66
63 16 10 76 41 70 19 93 31 05 52 41
56 08 27 29 47 72 78 35 24 77 05 54
74 62 46 99 88 43 95 35 63 25 60 03
39 19 21 51 09 19 88 92 59 70 48 26
81 52 43 86 58 86 04 52 51 61 10 64
03 90 46 52 78 77 65 73 18 41 14 94
```

Discount factors

Discount rate	1	2	3	4	Number of years 5	6	7	8	9	10
0.5%	0.9950	0.9901	0.9851	0.9802	0.9754	0.9705	0.9657	0.9609	0.9561	0.9513
1.0%	0.9901	0.9803	0.9706	0.9610	0.9515	0.9420	0.9327	0.9235	0.9143	0.9053
1.5%	0.9852	0.9707	0.9563	0.9422	0.9283	0.9145	0.9010	0.8877	0.8746	0.8617
2.0%	0.9804	0.9612	0.9423	0.9238	0.9057	0.8880	0.8706	0.8535	0.8368	0.8203
2.5%	0.9756	0.9518	0.9286	0.9060	0.8839	0.8623	0.8413	0.8207	0.8007	0.7812
3.0%	0.9709	0.9426	0.9151	0.8885	0.8626	0.8375	0.8131	0.7894	0.7664	0.7441
3.5%	0.9662	0.9335	0.9019	0.8714	0.8420	0.8135	0.7860	0.7594	0.7337	0.7089
4.0%	0.9615	0.9246	0.8890	0.8548	0.8219	0.7903	0.7599	0.7307	0.7026	0.6756
4.5%	0.9569	0.9157	0.8763	0.8386	0.8025	0.7679	0.7348	0.7032	0.6729	0.6439
5.0%	0.9524	0.9070	0.8638	0.8227	0.7835	0.7462	0.7107	0.6768	0.6446	0.6139
5.5%	0.9479	0.8985	0.8516	0.8072	0.7651	0.7252	0.6874	0.6516	0.6176	0.5854
6.0%	0.9434	0.8900	0.8396	0.7921	0.7473	0.7050	0.6651	0.6274	0.5919	0.5584
6.5%	0.9390	0.8817	0.8278	0.7773	0.7299	0.6853	0.6435	0.6042	0.5674	0.5327
7.0%	0.9346	0.8734	0.8163	0.7629	0.7130	0.6663	0.6227	0.5820	0.5439	0.5083
7.5%	0.9302	0.8653	0.8050	0.7488	0.6966	0.6480	0.6028	0.5607	0.5216	0.4852
8.0%	0.9259	0.8573	0.7938	0.7350	0.6806	0.6302	0.5835	0.5403	0.5002	0.4632
8.5%	0.9217	0.8495	0.7829	0.7216	0.6650	0.6129	0.5649	0.5207	0.4799	0.4423
9.0%	0.9174	0.8417	0.7722	0.7084	0.6499	0.5963	0.5470	0.5019	0.4604	0.4224
9.5%	0.9132	0.8340	0.7617	0.6956	0.6352	0.5801	0.5298	0.4838	0.4418	0.4035
10.0%	0.9091	0.8264	0.7513	0.6830	0.6209	0.5645	0.5132	0.4665	0.4241	0.3855
10.5%	0.9050	0.8190	0.7412	0.6707	0.6070	0.5493	0.4971	0.4499	0.4071	0.3684
11.0%	0.9009	0.8116	0.7312	0.6587	0.5935	0.5346	0.4817	0.4339	0.3909	0.3522
11.5%	0.8969	0.8044	0.7214	0.6470	0.5803	0.5204	0.4667	0.4186	0.3754	0.3367
12.0%	0.8929	0.7972	0.7118	0.6355	0.5674	0.5066	0.4523	0.4039	0.3606	0.3220
12.5%	0.8889	0.7901	0.7023	0.6243	0.5549	0.4933	0.4385	0.3897	0.3464	0.3079
13.0%	0.8850	0.7831	0.6931	0.6133	0.5428	0.4803	0.4251	0.3762	0.3329	0.2946
13.5%	0.8811	0.7763	0.6839	0.6026	0.5309	0.4678	0.4121	0.3631	0.3199	0.2819
14.0%	0.8772	0.7695	0.6750	0.5921	0.5194	0.4556	0.3996	0.3506	0.3075	0.2697
14.5%	0.8734	0.7628	0.6662	0.5818	0.5081	0.4438	0.3876	0.3385	0.2956	0.2582
15.0%	0.8696	0.7561	0.6575	0.5718	0.4972	0.4323	0.3759	0.3269	0.2843	0.2472
15.5%	0.8658	0.7496	0.6490	0.5619	0.4865	0.4212	0.3647	0.3158	0.2734	0.2367
16.0%	0.8621	0.7432	0.6407	0.5523	0.4761	0.4104	0.3538	0.3050	0.2630	0.2267
16.5%	0.8584	0.7368	0.6324	0.5429	0.4660	0.4000	0.3433	0.2947	0.2530	0.2171
17.0%	0.8547	0.7305	0.6244	0.5337	0.4561	0.3898	0.3332	0.2848	0.2434	0.2080
17.5%	0.8511	0.7243	0.6164	0.5246	0.4465	0.3800	0.3234	0.2752	0.2342	0.1994
18.0%	0.8475	0.7182	0.6086	0.5158	0.4371	0.3704	0.3139	0.2660	0.2255	0.1911
18.5%	0.8439	0.7121	0.6010	0.5071	0.4280	0.3612	0.3048	0.2572	0.2170	0.1832
19.0%	0.8403	0.7062	0.5934	0.4987	0.4190	0.3521	0.2959	0.2487	0.2090	0.1756
19.5%	0.8368	0.7003	0.5860	0.4904	0.4104	0.3434	0.2874	0.2405	0.2012	0.1684
20.0%	0.8333	0.6944	0.5787	0.4823	0.4019	0.3349	0.2791	0.2326	0.1938	0.1615

Appendix 3 *Mathematical and statistical formulae used in this book*

Chapter 1 *Index Numbers*

Laspeyres' index

$$\frac{\sum p_n q_0}{\sum p_0 q_0} \times 100$$

Paasche's index

$$\frac{\sum p_n q_n}{\sum p_0 q_n} \times 100$$

Chapter 2 *Investment Appraisal*

Average Rate of Return

$$ARR = \frac{\text{Average profits}}{\text{Initial capital}} \times 100\%$$

Compound interest formula:

$$P_n = P_0 \left(1 + \frac{r}{100}\right)^n$$

Present value formula:

$$P_0 = P_n \times \frac{1}{\left(1 + \frac{r}{100}\right)^n}$$

Net Present Value

NPV = sum of discounted cash flows - initial investment

IRR calculation (formula for linear interpolation)

$$IRR = \frac{N_1 r_2 - N_2 r_1}{N_1 - N_2}$$

Chapter 3 *Time Series Analysis*

The additive model

$$Y = T + S + C + R$$

The multiplicative model

$$Y = T \times S \times C \times R$$

Error statistics

$$MAD = \frac{\sum |\text{errors}|}{n}$$

$$MSE = \frac{\sum (\text{errors})^2}{n}$$

Exponential smoothing:

Next forecast = Last forecast + a x error in last forecast

Chapter 6 Inventory Control

Economic Order Quantity

$$EOQ = \sqrt{\frac{2CD}{h}}$$

Index